Marshmallows
Homemade Gourmet Treats

Eileen Talanian

Gibbs Smith, Publisher
TO ENRICH AND INSPIRE HUMANKIND
Salt Lake City | Charleston | Santa Fe | Santa Barbara

First Edition

12 11 10 09 08   5 4 3 2 1

Published by

Gibbs Smith, Publisher

P.O. Box 667

Layton, Utah 84041

Orders: 1.800.835.4993

www.gibbs-smith.com

Cover design by Natalie Peirce

Interior design by Kurt Wahlner

Food Styling by Dan Macey

Printed and bound in China

Library of Congress Cataloging-in-Publication Data

Talanian, Eileen.
   Marshmallows : homemade gourmet treats / Eileen Talanian. -- 1st ed.
      p. cm.
   Includes index.
   ISBN-13: 978-1-4236-0249-1
   ISBN-10: 1-4236-0249-8
   1. Cookery (Marshmallow) 2. Marshmallow. I. Title.

TX799.T28 2008

641.8'53--dc22

                                    2007035085

To my family, without whom
my life would be much less sweet.

Acknowledgements

I want to thank Clare Pelino, my agent, for her hard work and kind personality, and Suzanne Gibbs Taylor, editorial vice president of Gibbs Smith, Publisher, who took a chance with this book. Hollie Keith, my editor, asked several important questions that made this a better cookbook. My friend Marlys Connor spent many days testing marshmallow recipes at varying high altitudes, and I truly appreciate her hard work and advice. Courtney Winston, the photographer, and Dan Macey, the food stylist, composed and shot handsome photos for the book, and were genuinely fun to work with. And, of course, I cannot forget my family and friends, especially Corinne and Arnold Johnson, and Anne Galbally and her beautiful daughters and sweet husband, who ate enough marshmallows to feed an army, or maybe two. Thank you all for helping to make this book possible.

Contents

Introduction

Making a batch of marshmallows is so simple you'll kick yourself for not having done it sooner. It's always been a mystery to me that people don't make marshmallows at home. It's fast, it's easy, and it's fun. So why isn't everyone making marshmallows?

While I was working on a marshmallow issue for my Web site, I made dozens of batches while developing the recipes. Loaded up with hundreds of marshmallows from my endeavors, I delivered bags of assorted flavors to my friends, and received the same reaction from every one of them: "You *made* these at *home?* These are delicious! I didn't know you could make marshmallows at home!" So that was it: people don't make marshmallows because they don't know they can. They have no idea it's so easy.

It's no secret that Americans love marshmallows—we consume more than 90 million pounds a year. We eat them in ice cream, cookies, fudge, candy bars, and s'mores. We add them to hot chocolate. We enjoy them out of hand, roast them over campfires, and use them to decorate birthday cakes.

As adults become more interested in the nostalgic foods of our childhoods, we're making them ourselves, but with higher-quality, more wholesome, and vastly more interesting ingredients than what the mass producers use. Homemade marshmallows are no different. The basic recipe uses just 6 ingredients: unflavored gelatin, water, cane sugar, cane sugar syrup, salt, and vanilla. Pure and simple. No additives, no chemical preservatives. And marshmallows can be mixed and molded in 30 to 40 minutes.

But the big surprise is how easy it is to make them in a myriad of flavors. If you want, you can replace some or all of the water with juice, liqueur, wine, or any other liquid. You can replace the sugar syrup with honey or molasses, infuse the marshmallows with spices or herbs, or add freshly made or frozen fruit puree or natural flavorings.

This book gives you all the information you need to create your own homemade marshmallows, marshmallow fluff, and even cute little "peepers" in dozens of unique and delicious flavors. You'll find step-by-step instructions for making basic marsh-mallows and marshmallow fluff, along with ideas for using them in amusing ways.

Baking has been a lifelong passion for me, including ownership of an award-winning bakery, which I have since sold, and I've included some of the recipes my family and friends love most for you to serve with your marshmallows and fluff. If you have questions, please visit my Web site at www.HomemadeGourmetMarshmallows.com and send me an e-mail. Have fun experimenting with the simple recipes in this book, and enjoy making homemade marshmallows and marshmallow fluff in a variety of versatile forms. Just remember to share!

Discovering Marshmallows and Where They Came From

Marshmallows are made from unflavored gelatin, the hot sugar syrup that is combined with it, and air that is whipped in. As the gelatin sets, it supports the air pockets that have formed within the elastic syrup, providing the structure needed to maintain a fluffy texture.

Marshmallows aren't a modern invention; they've been with us in various forms for thousands of years. The ancient Egyptians made them by combining honey with the sap from the root of the marsh mallow plant. But unlike today, enjoyment of marshmallows back then was limited to Egyptian royalty, and they were offered as gifts to the gods.

In the early nineteenth century, marshmallow candy was given to children with sore throats in Western countries, but by the middle of the century, the marsh mallow sap was replaced with gelatin, and the candy no longer possessed healing powers.

As the world became more industrialized, extruding machines made mass production possible in the middle of the twentieth century, and marshmallows became a popular confection throughout the United States.

Learning about Equipment

Heavy-Duty Electric Stand Mixer with a Wire Whisk or Flat Beater

It is best to use a heavy-duty stand mixer to make homemade marshmallows. Even the most powerful hand mixers might overheat during the beating process, and many hand-mixer motors will burn out when used to beat the thick, sticky batter. A few flavors require 15 or more minutes beating time, which is difficult to do with a hand mixer. Use the wire whisk attachment if you have one for both marshmallows and marshmallow fluff. If you don't have a wire whisk for your stand mixer, you can use a paddle attachment. Your marshmallows will still be wonderful, just not quite as fluffy.

Candy Thermometer

Standard instant-read and meat thermometers don't have the temperature range necessary to track the heat of the syrup as it rises to the specific temperature required for marshmallow making. Use a candy thermometer for best results. The least expensive is a mercury thermometer encased with a metal clip that attaches to the saucepan to keep it upright. Another style, more expensive but much easier to read, is a mercury thermometer attached to a flat metal casing with a metal clip to hold it upright in the pan. The most accurate, but more expensive, is a battery-powered digital thermometer that registers the temperature on an LCD display. It can alert you with a beep when the correct temperature has been reached, in case you become distracted. It can be used for a number of cooking projects, so buying one is a good investment.

Heavy Saucepans

A 4-quart saucepan with a heavy bottom and sides should be used for making most of the marshmallow recipes from this book, and the same in a 2-quart size for most of the fluff recipes. If the pan is smaller than specified in the recipe, the cooked base might boil over, and if it's too large, the base might not be high enough in the pan to register its temperature on the candy thermometer.

Flexible Heatproof Spatula

Having one or more heatproof silicone spatulas helps in stirring the hot base, scraping the sticky marshmallow batter out of the mixer bowl, and smoothing the top of the marshmallow slab.

Measuring Cups and Spoons

You'll need a set of dry measuring cups, at least one 2-cup liquid measuring cup, and a set of measuring spoons to make recipes from this book.

Pan for Molding the Marshmallows

Unless otherwise indicated, the marshmallow batters in this book will fit into a 9 x 13-inch rectangular baking pan, or an 11 x 15-inch jelly roll/cookie sheet (the kind with sides). If you don't have either of those pans, don't despair. You can spread the batter into any pan or mold large enough to hold it; more than one pan or mold; or onto any flat, smooth, prepared surface, to whatever thickness you like.

The batter is extremely sticky, so any pan or surface you use for the marshmallow batter should be either dusted generously with the coating mixture or very lightly oiled.

Marshmallow Cutting Tools

Marshmallows can be cut using a lightly oiled pizza wheel, chef's knife, pair of kitchen scissors, or cheese wire. (You can make your own cheese wire by wrapping the ends of a thin, smooth, rustproof wire or filament around pencils. The wire will cut through the marshmallow, and the pencils serve as handles.) I prefer using a pizza wheel, which zips right through the marshmallow. The one I use is made by All-Clad, and is a sturdy stainless steel instrument with a large wheel that gives me good control while cutting the marshmallows quickly and with ease.

Kitchen Scale

You can certainly manage without a kitchen scale; however, if you can afford one, they are easy to use and reduce the need for measuring cups, so there are fewer dishes to wash. There is a scale on the market, the Pana made by Escali, which converts the weight of ingredients into cups or tablespoons.

Equipment for Making Fancy Marshmallows

In addition to the equipment listed above, you might want to have an assortment of sharp cookie cutters or a piping bag and tips to make fancier marshmallow shapes and fun projects or gifts. Silicone molds, fancy baking pans, and individual cake pans in special shapes can all be used as marshmallow molds, as long as they are oiled to prevent sticking.

Learning about Ingredients

When making your own marshmallows, you can control what goes into them so they are free of artificial ingredients and preservatives, and are uniquely flavored. Because marshmallows are delicately flavored, it's important that you use high-quality ingredients.

Gelatin

The ingredient that gives marshmallows their popular texture is *unflavored* gelatin, which can be found in most grocery stores in granulated form. I used Knox brand granulated unflavored gelatin to test the recipes in this book. Using a vegan or kosher gelatin substitute may provide very different results. You can use most gelatin sheets in these recipes by substituting them in equal weight for the granulated variety. A tablespoon of powdered gelatin weighs about 7 grams. Soften the gelatin sheets in cold water, dissolve them in the cooked base, and proceed with the recipe.

Granulated gelatin is usually sold in pre-measured packets of *approximately* 2 1/2 teaspoons. Their weight is an *average* weight, and not every packet will contain exactly the same amount of gelatin as another. You'll need to empty the packets into a small dish and then measure the gelatin for the recipes.

Gelatin is first mixed with a cold liquid for 5 or more minutes to soften it and separate the granules (referred to in this book as blooming the gelatin), and then mixed with a hot liquid to dissolve it so the gelatin doesn't form clumps. Don't skip this step. Depending on the recipe, the softened gelatin mixture may be runny or very stiff. Don't be alarmed by this difference from one recipe to another.

Cane Sugar Syrup vs. Light Corn Syrup

Most marshmallow recipes call for light corn syrup, which helps to eliminate sugar crystallization when making marshmallows, because it contains invert sugar molecules that stabilize regular sugar molecules. I've developed the recipes in this book using a simple-to-make syrup, that I call Marshmallow Syrup, consisting of cane sugar, water, and cream of tartar, a naturally occurring acid that is a by-product of winemaking (readily available in the

baking section of grocery stores). The cream of tartar acts as a catalyst in the reaction between sugar and water to form an invert sugar, stabilizing the sugar molecules in the marshmallows the same way corn syrup would. It takes about half an hour to make a 1-quart batch of the syrup, and it will keep at room temperature for up to 2 months. The recipe is on page 26.

Marshmallows made with Marshmallow Syrup are fluffier than those made with corn syrup and are not gummy, and the flavors are cleaner. Because of the health questions surrounding the use of corn syrup, I see no reason to use it when making marshmallows, although you can substitute light corn syrup for the cane sugar syrup, if you prefer.

Cane Sugar vs. Beet Sugar

All of these recipes were tested using pure granulated *cane* sugar. Unless the bag says "pure cane sugar," you may be getting beet sugar, which has been reported to react differently in many recipes.[1]

1. "Sugar, Sugar: Cane and Beet Share the Same Chemistry but Act Differently in the Kitchen," Miriam Morgan, *San Francisco Chronicle,* March 31, 1999.

Water

I know what you're thinking: How silly is it to discuss water as an ingredient in a cookbook? Well, marshmallows have only a few ingredients, so it's vitally important that you don't use water that has an off-flavor or odor. If you use well water in your home, for instance, the flavor of sulfur or other naturally occurring minerals in the water may come through in the marshmallows. Use bottled water instead, if that is the case.

Fruits

Fruit to be used in marshmallows should be fresh, locally grown, in season, and very ripe, but not past its prime. If the fruit flavor you desire isn't in season when you make marshmallows, use the frozen variety of that fruit instead; your marshmallows will have a significantly better flavor.

Fruits that are especially suited to marshmallow making are strawberries, raspberries, blackberries, bananas, peaches, nectarines, apricots, mangoes, and plums. For fruits that are grainy in texture, like pears or apples, it's best to use juice or nectar.

Do not use these fresh fruits raw in marshmallows: figs, kiwifruits, papayas, pineapples, guavas, mangoes, or prickly pears. Also, do not use fresh gingerroot. These items contain a protease enzyme

that destroys the protein in gelatin, preventing it from gelling, or causing the gelatin to break down after the marshmallows are made. To deactivate the enzyme in all of these fruits *except* kiwifruit, peel and chop the fruit and then bring it to a boil, simmering it for 5 minutes. Do not use kiwifruit, raw or cooked, to make marshmallows. I did, however, have good luck with uncooked frozen mango chunks.

You can also use unsweetened fruit purees such as the top-quality Perfect Purees brand (see resources, page 173) for any of the marshmallow or fluff recipes calling for pureed fruit.

Cocoa

There are 2 types of unsweetened cocoa: natural and Dutch processed. Natural cocoa provides a deep chocolate flavor, is slightly acidic, and reacts with baking soda to cause baked goods to rise. Dutch-processed cocoa has a milder flavor, is reddish-brown, and is alkalized, neutralizing the acid in cocoa. Baking powder is often used to leaven baked goods that are made with Dutch-processed cocoa.

Buy a high-quality natural cocoa, such as Ghirardelli, or one of the great choices from King Arthur or Penzeys Spices (see resources, page 173).

Making Marshmallows in High Altitudes

If you live in a high-altitude area, you'll need to make some adjustments to the temperatures in the marshmallow and fluff recipes as follows: fill a saucepan with water, insert a candy thermometer into the pan, and place it over high heat. Bring the water to a boil, carefully noting the temperature at which the water boils. (Once the water comes to a full boil, the temperature won't continue to rise.) Subtract that number from 212 (the Fahrenheit temperature at which water boils at sea level). Write the resulting number down in the front of this book so you won't forget it. Subtract that number from any of the temperatures used in making marshmallows, marshmallow syrup, or marshmallow fluff. For example, if water boils in your area at 203 degrees F instead of 212 degrees F, you would deduct the difference (9 degrees) from the temperatures given in those recipes.

Using Tips
and Techniques

Be Smart Before You Start!

You need to be organized when you make marshmallows. Read through the recipe to be certain you know what you are expected to do. Then assemble all of the ingredients, *prepped and measured,* in your work area before you begin. Chefs refer to this as a *mise en place,* which means setting everything in place. It will make the process easier and keep you from making silly mistakes. Follow the recipes to get the best results.

Measuring Accurately

It doesn't take any extra time to measure ingredients accurately than it does to be sloppy about it—but it can cause the marshmallows or fluff to fail. In this book, liquids have been measured in measuring cups designed for liquids; dry ingredients have been measured in cups designed for dry ingredients and are level measurements. Use a straight-edged instrument, such as a table knife or icing spatula, to level the ingredients in the dry measuring cups.

No Stopping Now

Once you start making marshmallows or marshmallow fluff, you must continue until you're finished. Marshmallows are easy to make, but they won't forgive you if you leave them to do something else, and there isn't any time to dillydally during the process. Once the marshmallow batter is finished being beaten, immediately start scraping the batter out of the bowl onto a lightly oiled baking sheet or one dusted with a coating mixture, or transfer it to a piping bag. Don't stop to get every last bit of batter from the bowl because you will lose precious time before the batter starts to set. The gelatin will start to set soon after you turn off the mixer.

Dealing with a Sticky Mess

Marshmallow batter is amazingly sticky. It will stubbornly fasten to any surface it touches that is not lightly coated with oil or dusted with a coating mixture—including your clothing, hair, and body. Fortunately, cleanup is easy because everything dissolves in warm water. As soon as you have poured the hot base into the mixer bowl, turn on the mixer, then fill the saucepan with warm water and let it sit until you are finished making and spreading the batter. Once the batter has been smoothed, wash the bowl, beater, and utensils with warm soapy water.

Using a Piping Bag and Decorating Tube

Piping bags and tips are available in kitchen shops and many discount and grocery stores. If you've never used a piping bag, it's a good idea to practice ahead of time if you will be piping marshmallows for a special event. Make a marshmallow batter and fill the piping bag half full. Twist the open end of the bag so the twist is snugly against the marshmallow batter and practice piping onto any washable coated surface. Hold the bag so the twist is in the crease between your thumb and forefinger; squeeze the bag with your hand to force the batter onto the surface. When you have piped the amount you want, stop squeezing the bag, and lift it from the piped marshmallow. As you pipe, twist the bag every so often to keep pressure on the contents, and place your other hand near the tip of the bag to keep it steady. It shouldn't take you long to get the hang of it, and you can eat all of the shapes you made while practicing, so there's no waste.

Cutting Marshmallows

Marshmallows are very sticky until they are covered with a coating mixture or coated in chocolate shavings, coconut, or other material. For the best success, lightly coat the cutting utensil with oil. Keep in mind that the cutting instrument may need to be washed a few times during the process.

If you will be coating the marshmallows, spread the cutting surface with part of the coating mixture and turn the pan upside down over it to release the marshmallows. Cut the marshmallows into desired shapes and coat them on all sides. If you will not be coating them with a sugar mixture or other coating, turn them out onto a clean dry surface that has been sprayed with a nonstick coating and lightly wiped with a paper towel.

Making Marshmallow Cutouts

The marshmallow slab should not be taller than the height of the cookie cutter, or you won't be able to push the cutter all the way through the slab. Most often, if you spread the marshmallow batter into a lightly oiled 11 x 15 x 1-inch pan, the marshmallow slab will not be too high for the cutters.

Turn out the marshmallow slab onto a prepared surface. Lightly spray the surface of the cookie cutter or other cutting instrument and wipe it gently with a paper towel before you push it into the marshmallow slab. Wash off any marshmallow that sticks to the cutter and re-oil it before making another cut.

Curing Marshmallows

This is honestly the most difficult part of making marshmallows because you have to wait before you cut and eat your masterpieces. In order for the gelatin to set up, the marshmallow batter has to sit, uncovered, for at least 4 hours, and sometimes overnight, depending on the flavor. No work is involved in doing this, but anyone who is anxious to enjoy the goodies will find it hard to wait.

Coloring and Layering Marshmallows

Marshmallows are easily colored with gel food colorings. You only need a small amount of coloring for the results to be enormously festive. When you have finished beating the marshmallow batter, fish out a little food coloring gel from its container with a toothpick and dab it into the marshmallow with the mixer off. Turn the mixer back on and beat for a few seconds to blend the color. If you want to add more,

do so. Remember: you can always add more, but you cannot take it out once it's been mixed in.

Layered marshmallows can be made 2 ways. You can make a batch or a half-batch of marshmallow and spread it into a prepared pan and then make another batch and spread it over the first. This can be done as many times, for as many layers, as you desire. You can also make a batch of marshmallow and quickly divide it into 2 parts, putting 1 part in another bowl and leaving 1 part in the mixing bowl. Add 1 color to the mixing bowl, beating to mix it in, and whisk the color into the other part. Then spread them in layers into a prepared pan.

Another way to make beautifully layered marshmallows is to make them in fruit flavors of different colors, layering them as each is finished.

Storing Marshmallows

Put your cut or shaped marshmallows into a container with a loose-fitting lid, or in an airtight plastic container, leaving one corner loosened. Marshmallows will dry out if left uncovered, but will have a longer life if they are able to get just a little air while being stored. Separate the layers of marshmallows with wax paper or parchment.

Some marshmallow varieties need to be refrigerated, and if so, it's specified in the recipe.

How Many Marshmallows Will I Get?

All of the marshmallow recipes in this book can be spread into a 9 x 13 x 2-inch baking pan, or an 11 x 15 x 1-inch jelly roll pan/baking sheet unless otherwise stated. You may use any other size pan(s) you prefer, keeping in mind that the broader the pan, the thinner the marshmallows will be. How you cut them and what size pan you use will determine how many marshmallows each recipe yields. To give you an idea of what to expect, a batch that is put into a 9 x 13-inch pan and cut into 1-inch squares will yield 117 marshmallows.

NOTE:

You can make a half batch of any of the marshmallow recipes in this book. Be sure to use a smaller 2-quart saucepan if you do so.

Making Basic Marshmallows

As long as you follow the directions, the marshmallows will turn out fluffy and delicious, and your family and friends will be amazed that you made such wonderful marshmallows in your home. The flavors that are covered in this section—vanilla, honey, and molasses—will give you a fundamental understanding of the process involved. You'll use these recipes as the base for other recipes in the book, and for developing flavors of your own. Once you see how easy it is, you won't hesitate to try the more interesting flavors in the following chapters, as well as some combinations of your own invention.

Marshmallows coated with brightly colored sugars.

Marshmallow Syrup

Makes about 1 quart

Here is an easy-to-make homemade cane sugar syrup to use for the recipes in this book. It takes about 30 minutes to make approximately 1 quart, which will keep in a covered jar for up to 2 months at room temperature. This recipe can be doubled or tripled if you are going to be making a lot of marshmallows or fluff; just be sure to use a pan large enough to allow for the ingredients to boil if you increase the recipe. If you don't allow the syrup to cool for 15 minutes before ladling it into jars, it will crystallize.

2 cups water

5 ⅓ cups granulated cane sugar

1 teaspoon cream of tartar

Pinch of salt

NOTE:

The syrup will be very thick once it cools. To use it, microwave for 2 minutes on high power, or place the jar in a pan of hot water over low heat until it can be poured easily. Do not stir the syrup.

Place the ingredients in a heavy 4-quart pan, stirring gently with a heatproof spatula until the sugar is moistened. Bring to a boil over medium-high heat, and cover the pan for 2 minutes to allow steam to wash any sugar crystals from the sides of the pan. Then uncover the pan, insert a candy thermometer, and increase the heat to high. *Do not stir it at all once you have removed the lid* or the syrup will crystallize as it cools. Continue cooking until it reaches 240 degrees F. Remove from the heat and let the syrup cool for 15 minutes. Ladle it into clean jars and attach the lids.

Store it at room temperature for up to 2 months. If the syrup begins to form crystals at the bottom of the jar, don't be alarmed; pour out the amount of syrup you need when you use it, without scraping the jar. Discard any crystallized part that is left in the jar.

Basic Marshmallow Coating

MAKES ABOUT 2 CUPS

If what you prefer is a simple coating for your marshmallows, this is it. You can use potato starch or rice flour in place of the cornstarch, if you prefer. Mass-produced marshmallows, like the kind found in the candy aisle of a standard supermarket, are coated only with cornstarch. I prefer a combination of 1 part cornstarch to 3 parts confectioners' sugar, but you can adjust this ratio to suit your own taste, or simply use plain cornstarch.

1 1/2 cups confectioners' sugar

1/2 cup cornstarch

Sift the sugar and cornstarch together, or put them into a food processor and pulse until there are no lumps. Store the coating indefinitely in an airtight container.

Coating Variations

One way to easily vary the flavor of a simple marshmallow recipe is by adding spices, freeze-dried fruit, or other ingredients to the coating mixture. Make these in the same way as the Basic Marshmallow Coating.

Vanilla Coating

MAKES ABOUT 2 CUPS

When you use a vanilla bean to infuse a syrup or custard, don't throw it away afterwards. Wash it off, dry it completely, and put it in an airtight container with the confectioners' sugar and cornstarch mixture from the Basic Marshmallow Coating recipe to make Vanilla Coating.

Fruit Powder

MAKES ABOUT 2 CUPS

Don't use regular dried fruits to make this because they won't work. It must
be the dry, brittle freeze-dried type. You can find the freeze-dried fruits at
Whole Foods Markets and health-food stores, or on the Internet (see
resources, page 173).

Add 2 tablespoons freeze-dried fruit, or to taste, to the Basic Marshmallow
Coating recipe, and completely pulverize the mixture in a food processor.

Gingerbread Coating

MAKES ABOUT 2 CUPS

My family loves this powder as the coating for Molasses Marshmallows because
they think the combination tastes like a mild gingerbread. You can adjust the
amount or variety of spices in this coating to suit your taste. Try adding a $1/2$ tea-
spoonful or so of ancho chile powder to provide a slight kick to the warm spices.

Add $1 1/2$ teaspoons ginger, 1 teaspoon cinnamon, and $3/4$ teaspoon cloves to
the Basic Marshmallow Coating recipe.

Cinnamon Coating

MAKES ABOUT 2 CUPS

You can use this to coat a number of flavored marshmallows. When you make
it, use Saigon (or Vietnamese) cinnamon because it has a much deeper, more
aromatic flavor than regular cinnamon. It's sold in most grocery stores.

Add 2 to 3 teaspoons ground Saigon (or Vietnamese) cinnamon to the Basic
Marshmallow Coating recipe.

Cocoa Coating

MAKES ABOUT 2 1/2 CUPS

Adding cocoa to the coating mixture provides a light chocolate taste to marshmallows. The darker the cocoa, the better the coating will look on your marshmallows. Penzeys Spices sells a lovely dark Dutch cocoa, and King Arthur Flour sells something they call Black Cocoa (see resources, page 173), which is extremely dark.

1 1/2 cups confectioners' sugar

1/2 cup or more, to taste, unsweetened natural cocoa, as dark as you can find

1/2 cup cornstarch

Sift the ingredients together, or put them into a food processor and pulse until there are no lumps. Store the coating indefinitely in an airtight container.

Cocoa-Ancho Chile Coating

MAKES ABOUT 2 1/2 CUPS

You can enhance the taste of Cocoa Coating by adding a bit of ancho chile powder. It provides a surprise hint of warmth but won't jolt you out of your chocolate reverie.

1 1/2 cups confectioners' sugar

1/2 cup unsweetened natural cocoa, as dark as you can find

1/2 cup cornstarch

2 teaspoons ancho chile powder

Sift the ingredients together, or put them into a food processor and pulse until there are no lumps. Store the coating indefinitely in an airtight container.

Green Tea Coating

MAKES ABOUT 2 CUPS

Add 1 to 2 tablespoons maccha green tea powder to the Basic Marshmallow
Coating recipe.

Citrus Coating

MAKES ABOUT 2 CUPS

Add 1 to 2 packets True Lemon or True Lime powder (available in grocery stores)
to the Basic Marshmallow Coating recipe.

Long Pepper Coating

MAKES ABOUT 2 CUPS

Long pepper (see resources, page 173) is a member of the same family as black
pepper, but it has a sweet spice component that provides a delicious and interesting flavor. To use it, crush the pepper rods coarsely, and finely grind them with a
pepper grinder.

Add 1 teaspoon finely ground long pepper to the Basic Marshmallow
Coating recipe.

NOTE:

Additional coating ideas include shredded or flaked coconut (toasted or plain), shaved or
ground chocolate, finely chopped nuts, multicolored sprinkles, brightly colored sugars, plain
cornstarch, mini chocolate chips, chopped dried fruit, and cinnamon sugar.

Making Your First Batch of Marshmallows

It should take you about 45 minutes to make your first batch of marshmallows, and less time as you become more familiar with the process. Basically, marshmallow making is broken down into these parts:

- **Marshmallow Syrup:** A homemade invert sugar syrup that helps to control crystallization.

- **The base:** This is the combination of Marshmallow Syrup, cane sugar, water, and, occasionally, other ingredients cooked to a specific temperature.

- **The bloom:** Before granulated gelatin can be used in a recipe, it must first be softened, or "bloomed," in a *cold* liquid so the crystals are separated and don't form lumps. Flavoring ingredients might be added to the bloom in some recipes.

- **Additional flavoring:** Certain flavorings can't be included in the cooked base or the bloom, so they're added at another time in the recipe and are listed separately in the ingredients list.

- **The marshmallow batter:** This refers to the base and bloom mixture that is poured into the bowl, beaten, and then spread into a pan, molded, or piped into shapes.

Vanilla Marshmallows

Homemade marshmallows are like the ones in the stores, only much, much better, with a clean vanilla flavor and creamy texture. They're great in hot chocolate, or eaten out of hand, and terrific in s'mores because they melt into a creamy mass. Be sure to try the dessert recipes starting on page 110, where you can find dozens of uses for your homemade marshmallows.

I've included a lot of detail in this first marshmallow recipe to make things as clear and easy as possible. Refer back to this recipe when making other flavors if you forget any of the details.

For the bloom:

1/2 cup + 2 tablespoons cold water

1 1/2 tablespoons pure vanilla extract

3 tablespoons unflavored gelatin

For the base:

3/4 cup water

1 1/4 cups Marshmallow Syrup
   (page 26)

Pinch salt

1 1/2 cups granulated cane sugar

Dulce de Leche Marshmallows,
Chocolate Chip Marshmallows,
and Vanilla Marshmallows.

Spray the bottom and sides of a 9 x 13 x 2-inch or 11 x 15 x 1-inch pan or another mold you will be using for the marshmallow batter with a pan coating such as Pam, and wipe it lightly with a paper towel, leaving only a thin film of oil.

Make the bloom. Measure the cold water into a measuring cup and add the vanilla. Place the gelatin into a small bowl and pour the water and vanilla over it, stirring with a whisk or fork until there are no lumps. Set the bowl near the stove.

Make the base. Place the water, Marshmallow Syrup, salt, and sugar, in that order, into a 4-quart pan. Bring the mixture to a boil over medium-high heat. Then place a lid on the pan and boil it, covered, for 2 minutes. This step is essential in order to eliminate sugar crystals on the side of the pan that may cause the marshmallows to crystallize.

Remove the lid, insert a candy thermometer, and continue boiling until the thermometer reaches 250 degrees F. *Do not stir the mixture once the lid has been removed.* Remove the thermometer and gently stir in the bloomed gelatin.

Pour the batter into the bowl of an electric stand mixer. Beat it on high speed for 10 to 12 minutes, using the wire whisk attachment or the paddle beater. It will take a little longer to beat with the paddle. You can cover the mixer with a clean kitchen towel for the first 3 or 4 minutes to avoid splattering hot liquid on yourself.

At first, the marshmallow batter will look very watery; as it beats, it will become thick, white, and glossy, and will increase in volume by two- to threefold. Remove the bowl from the mixer stand and spread the marshmallow batter into the prepared pan. Smooth the top with a spatula, or wet your hand and smooth the marshmallow with your palm. Let the pan set out at room temperature, uncovered, for at least 4 hours or overnight.

When you're ready to cut the marshmallows, prepare the cutting surface. Lightly sprinkle a work surface with the coating mixture you will be using. Ease the marshmallows away from the sides of the pan and flip the pan over, gently releasing the marshmallow slab onto the cutting surface. Cut into squares, or other shapes, or use cookie cutters to cut the marshmallow into fancy shapes. Toss the cut marshmallows in the coating mix, shaking off any excess coating.

Place the coated marshmallows in an airtight container, with wax paper between the layers, and leave a corner of the lid slightly ajar. The marshmallows will keep this way for up to 2 weeks at room temperature.

If you are dipping the marshmallows in chocolate, or using another coating such as coconut or sprinkles, or will not be coating the marshmallows, do not sprinkle a coating mixture on the cutting surface. Spray the surface with a nonstick coating instead, and lightly wipe off any excess, leaving only a thin film of oil. Cut them into the desired shapes and layer them in an airtight container, with a corner slightly ajar, and with lightly oiled parchment or wax paper between the layers.

Recommended coatings: any of the coating mixtures will go well with Vanilla Marshmallows.

Chocolate Chip Marshmallows

(See photo, page 32.)

Make Vanilla Marshmallows, cooking the base to 260 degrees F. When the batter is finished beating, remove the bowl from the stand and fold in 1 cup of high-quality mini chocolate chips. Spread the batter into the prepared pan, sprinkle it with another 3 tablespoons of mini chocolate chips, and allow it to cure for 4 hours or overnight. Recommended coatings: Basic, Cocoa, Vanilla.

Dulce de Leche Marshmallows

(See photo, page 32.)

You might think this combination would be too sweet, but the dulce de leche actually tempers the sweetness of the marshmallow. You can buy dulce de leche in Hispanic markets, gourmet shops, or well-stocked grocery stores.

Make Vanilla Marshmallows. While the marshmallow batter is beating, soften 1 cup of store-bought Dulce de Leche in the microwave until it is thin enough to pour. Spread half of the batter into the prepared pan, and drizzle $1/2$ cup Dulce de Leche over the batter. Using a table knife, swirl the Dulce de Leche into the batter. Repeat with the remaining batter and Dulce de Leche. Let the marshmallow cure overnight. Cut as desired and coat if you like, but no coating is really needed.

Honey Marshmallows

A true honey flavor comes out clearly in this recipe. Experiment with different honey varieties, like wild-flower or blackberry; every type has its own unique flavor. If you prefer a milder honey flavor, you can replace some of the honey with Marshmallow Syrup (see page 26). Be sure to use a large saucepan because the honey will boil up high.

For the bloom:

3 tablespoons unflavored gelatin

1/2 cup + 2 tablespoons cold water

For the base:

3/4 cup water

1 1/4 cups honey

Pinch salt

1 1/2 cups granulated cane sugar

Honey Marshmallows with Candied Ginger

Before you spread the Honey Marshmallow batter into the pan, fold in 2 tablespoons (or to taste) finely chopped candied ginger.
Recommended coatings: Basic, Gingerbread, Green Tea.

Prepare a pan by coating it with nonstick spray, then wiping it lightly with a paper towel so that only a thin film of oil remains.

Make the bloom. Place the gelatin into a small bowl and whisk in the water until there are no lumps. Set the bowl near the stove.

Make the base. Place the water, honey, salt, and sugar, in that order, into a 6-quart pan. Bring the mixture to a boil over medium-high heat, cover the pan, and boil the base for 2 minutes. Remove the lid, insert a candy thermometer, and continue boiling until the thermometer reaches 250 degrees F. *Do not stir the mixture once the lid has been removed.* Remove the thermometer and gently stir in the bloomed gelatin.

Pour the batter into the bowl of an electric stand mixer, beating on high speed for 10 to 12 minutes. You can cover the mixer with a clean kitchen towel for the first 3 or 4 minutes to avoid splattering hot liquid on yourself.

Remove the bowl from the mixer stand and spread the marsh-mallow batter into the prepared pan, smoothing the top. Let the pan set out at room temperature, uncovered, for at least 4 hours or overnight. Cut and coat as desired. The marshmallows will keep for up to 2 weeks at room temperature. Recommended coatings: Basic, Green Tea, Cinnamon, Gingerbread, Fruit Powder.

Molasses Marshmallows

The mild molasses flavor in these marshmallows marries well with spices. The marshmallows are especially good when coated with Gingerbread Coating mixture, and make a spicy addition to hot chocolate. If you prefer a more prominent molasses flavor, replace some of the Marshmallow Syrup with additional molasses.

For the bloom:

3 tablespoons unflavored gelatin

3/4 cup cold water

For the base:

1/2 cup water

1/2 cup molasses

2/3 cup Marshmallow Syrup
(page 26)

Pinch salt

1 1/4 cups granulated cane sugar

Prepare a pan by coating it with nonstick spray, then wiping it lightly with a paper towel so that only a thin film of oil remains.

Prepare the bloom. Place the gelatin in a small bowl and add the cold water, stirring with a small whisk or fork until the mixture is completely smooth. Set the bowl near the stove.

Place the base ingredients into a 4-quart pan. Bring the mixture to a boil over medium-high heat, cover the pan, and boil for 2 minutes. Remove the lid, insert a candy thermometer, and cook the base to 248 degrees F. *Do not stir the mixture once the lid has been removed.*

When the temperature of the base reaches 248 degrees F, turn off the heat, remove the thermometer, and add the bloomed gelatin to the pan, stirring gently. Pour the batter into the bowl of a stand mixer; gradually increase the speed to high, and beat for 10 minutes, placing a kitchen towel over the mixer for the first 3 minutes to avoid hot splatters.

Spread the batter into the prepared pan, smoothing the top. Set out the pan to room temperature, uncovered, for a few hours or overnight. Cut and coat as desired. Store the cut marshmallows in an airtight container for up to 1 1/2 weeks. Recommended coatings: Gingerbread, Basic.

Making Marshmallows
with Fruit Purees

The best fruits to use in marshmallows are those that have smooth flesh and intense flavors. If you're unable to obtain fresh, locally grown fruit that is in season, use frozen; you'll get a better marshmallow flavor if you do. Check the list on page 15 for fruits that need to be cooked before using them in recipes that contain gelatin.

Raspberry-Crème de Cassis Marshmallows

There's something truly sensuous about raspberries. Such a luxurious flavor and beautifully colored fruit calls out to be used in marshmallows. They pair well with Crème de Cassis, a black currant liqueur with a deep fruit flavor. Buy local in-season berries for this recipe; if you can't find them, use frozen raspberries without sugar. It will take two 10-ounce bags to make these spectacularly pink marshmallows.

For the raspberry puree:

20 ounces fresh or dry-frozen raspberries

For the bloom:

4 tablespoons unflavored gelatin

1/4 cup Crème de Cassis

1 cup raspberry puree at cool room
   temperature

For the base:

1/2 cup water

1 1/4 cups pureed raspberries

1 1/4 cups Marshmallow Syrup (page 26)

Pinch salt

2 cups granulated cane sugar

Prepare a pan by coating it with nonstick spray, then wiping it lightly with a paper towel so that only a thin film of oil remains.

Puree the raspberries in a food processor or blender. Pour the puree into a fine mesh strainer set over a bowl, and press it with a spoon to remove the seeds. Mix 1 cup of the puree in a bowl with the other bloom ingredients, whisking until there are no lumps. Set the bloom near the mixer.

Pour the remaining puree into a 6-quart saucepan. Add the other base ingredients and stir gently to moisten the sugar. Bring to a boil over medium heat, using a pastry brush dipped in water to wash down any crystals that form on the sides of the pan. *Do not cover the pan.* The raspberry base will boil up vigorously and could boil over if you do. *Do not stir the mixture once you have washed down the sides of the pan.* Insert a candy thermometer and cook the base to 240 degrees F. Remove the thermometer.

Pour the base into the bowl of a stand mixer *without scraping the bottom of the pan* and gently stir the bloom into it. Any seeds remaining in the puree will fall to the bottom of the pan during cooking. After pouring the batter into the mixer, add some water to the pan and place it over medium heat. The seeds can easily be loosened with a heatproof spatula and discarded. Gradually increase the mixer speed to high and beat the marshmallow batter for 12 minutes. You can cover the mixer with a clean kitchen towel for the first 3 or 4 minutes to avoid splattering hot liquid on yourself.

Spread the batter into the prepared pan and let it cure, uncovered, for at least 4 hours or overnight. Cut and coat as desired. Store the cut marshmallows in an airtight container, with a corner slightly ajar, for up to 10 days. Recommended coatings: Fruit Powder, Basic, Cocoa, ground or shaved chocolate, tempered chocolate.

Banana Marshmallows

Make sure the bananas you use are well covered with dark brown spots but not mushy. If they aren't ripe, your marshmallows will have no flavor and may turn grey; if too ripe, they may have a bitter flavor. The flavor develops more as the marshmallow sets, so allow for the marshmallow to cure overnight for a bright, fresh banana flavor. I used Looza brand banana nectar for this recipe.

For the base:

1/2 cup banana nectar or water

1 1/4 cups Marshmallow Syrup (page 26)

Pinch salt

1 1/2 cups granulated cane sugar

For the bloom:

3 or 4 medium to large bananas

4 tablespoons unflavored gelatin

1/2 teaspoon Fruit-Fresh, optional (available in well-stocked grocery stores)

Prepare a pan by coating it with nonstick spray, then wiping it lightly with a paper towel so that only a thin film of oil remains.

Place all of the base ingredients into a heavy 4-quart saucepan. Bring to a boil over medium heat, cover, and boil for 2 minutes. Remove the cover, insert a candy thermometer, and boil until the base reaches 260 degrees F. *Do not stir at all once you have removed the lid.*

When the base reaches 230 degrees F, make the bloom. Peel the bananas, place them in a bowl, mash them with a fork, and measure 1 1/2 cups; set aside any remaining for another use. Place the mashed banana, the gelatin, and the Fruit Fresh, if you are using it, into the work bowl of a food processor, pulsing until the mixture is a smooth paste.

When the base reaches 260 degrees F, turn off the heat, remove the thermometer, and add the bloom, stirring gently with a heatproof spatula. Pour the batter into the bowl of a stand mixer and gradually increase the speed to high. You can cover the mixer with a clean kitchen towel for the first 3 or 4 minutes to avoid splattering hot liquid on yourself. Beat for 14 minutes. Spread into the prepared pan and let cure, uncovered, overnight. Cut into desired shapes and coat. Store in an airtight container, with a corner slightly ajar, for up to 1 week. Recommended coatings: Basic, Cocoa, Gingerbread, Cinnamon, chocolate chips, ground or shaved chocolate.

Sweet Potato Spice Marshmallows

While not technically a fruit, sweet potatoes liven up all kinds of dishes with their deep orange color and sumptuous sugary taste. Look for brightly colored orange sweet potatoes, such as Jewel or Garnet, for this recipe. The Asian hot chili sauce adds a pleasant warmth to the sweet potato flavor. You can find it in Asian markets.

For the bloom:

1 cup mashed cooked
  sweet potato

1/2 cup cold water

1/4 to 1/2 teaspoon
  Asian hot chili sauce

4 tablespoons unflavored gelatin

For the base:

1/2 cup water

1 1/4 cups Marshmallow Syrup
  (page 26)

1/4 teaspoon salt

2 cups granulated cane sugar

Additional flavoring:

1/2 teaspoon ground ginger

1/4 teaspoon ground Saigon (or
  Vietnamese) cinnamon

Prepare a pan by coating it with nonstick spray, then wiping it lightly with a paper towel so that only a thin film of oil remains.

Prepare the bloom by pureeing the sweet potato, water, and hot chili sauce in a food processor. Add the gelatin and process until the mixture is smooth. Set the bloom aside near the stove.

Make the base. Place all of the ingredients for the base in a heavy 4-quart saucepan and bring the base to a boil. Cover the pan and continue boiling for 2 minutes. Remove the lid, insert a thermometer, and cook the base to 255 degrees F. *Do not stir the mixture once the lid has been removed.*

When the base reaches 255 degrees F, remove the pan from the heat and remove the thermometer. Stir the bloom into the base, pour the mixture into the bowl of a stand mixer, and gradually increase the speed to high. Cover the mixer with a clean kitchen towel for the first 3 or 4 minutes to avoid splattering hot liquid on yourself. Beat the marshmallow for a total of 10 minutes.

When there is 1 minute of beating left, add the ground ginger and cinnamon, and finish beating the batter. Spread it into the prepared pan and let the marshmallow cure for at least 4 hours or overnight. Cut and coat as desired and store the marshmallows in an airtight container, with a corner ajar, for up to 2 weeks. Recommended coatings: Basic, plain cornstarch, Long Pepper.

Strawberry Marshmallows

The deep colors and intense flavor of strawberries make them perfect ingredients for marshmallows. These marshmallows are a pretty pink color, and impart a fresh strawberry flavor. Don't use fresh strawberries unless you can get them locally in season—the out-of-season berries have no flavor and neither will your marshmallows if you use them. Use berries that have been frozen without sugar instead. These marshmallows are especially delicious when dipped in chocolate. This recipe requires a larger saucepan, because the berries boil up high.

For the bloom:

4 tablespoons unflavored gelatin

1 1/4 cups pureed strawberries at cool room temperature

For the base:

1/2 cup water

2/3 cup pureed strawberries

1 1/4 cups Marshmallow Syrup (page 26)

2 cups granulated cane sugar

Pinch salt

Prepare a pan by coating it with nonstick spray, then wiping it lightly with a paper towel so that only a thin film of oil remains.

Make the bloom. Place the gelatin in a small bowl and stir in the puréed strawberries until there are no lumps. Place the bowl near the stove.

Fill a cup with warm water and set it near the stove with a pastry brush. Place the base ingredients in a heavy 6-quart saucepan over medium heat. This base boils up high, so keep it over medium heat and watch closely. Do not cover the pan. Bring the mixture to a boil, using the pastry brush dipped in water to wash down the sides of the pan to dissolve any sugar crystals that may have accumulated there. *Do not stir the mixture once you have washed down the sides of the pan.* Insert a candy thermometer, and boil the mixture until the temperature reaches 250 degrees F.

Turn off the heat, remove the thermometer, and stir in the bloomed gelatin. Pour the batter into the bowl of a stand mixer and gradually increase the speed to high. Cover the mixer with a clean kitchen towel for the first 3 or 4 minutes to avoid splattering hot liquid on yourself. Beat the marshmallow for a total of 10 minutes.

Spread the mixture into the prepared pan and let it cure, uncovered, for at least 4 hours or overnight. Cut and coat the marshmallows as desired, and store them in an airtight container, with a corner ajar, for up to 2 weeks. Recommended coatings: Basic, Cocoa, Strawberry or Banana Fruit Powder.

Blackberry Marshmallows

The intense flavor of blackberries and their deep color work beautifully in marshmallows to produce a rich pink-violet hue and a scrumptious blackberry flavor. If you don't have access to fresh, locally grown blackberries that are in season, use blackberries that have been frozen without sugar.

Follow the recipe for Strawberry Marshmallows, substituting blackberry puree for the strawberry puree. Recommended coatings: Basic, Fruit Powder, coconut.

Passion Fruit Marshmallows

With such an unusual name, it's not surprising that passion fruit also has an unusual flavor. Its tart, delicately floral, citrus-pineapple, and almost-bitter flavor makes an unexpectedly pleasant marshmallow. This is not an inexpensive marshmallow to make; it's flavored with the Perfect Puree brand of passion fruit concentrate. But it is refreshing, uncommon, and quite enjoyable. For information on where to get Perfect Purees, see page 173.

Make the Strawberry Marshmallow recipe, substituting water for the strawberry puree in the base, and substituting passion fruit concentrate for the strawberry puree in the bloom. Recommended coatings: Basic, Fruit Powder, toasted coconut.

Pumpkin Marshmallows

Perfect for a surprise Thanksgiving treat for the kids, Pumpkin Marshmallows can be easily made a few days before the holiday. Serve them with hot apple cider.

Follow the Sweet Potato Marshmallow recipe, substituting pumpkin puree (*not* pumpkin pie mix, which contains a lot of other ingredients) for the sweet potatoes. Omit the hot chili sauce and replace the ground ginger and cinnamon with this combination: 1 1/2 teaspoons ground Saigon (or Vietnamese) cinnamon, 1/2 teaspoon ground ginger, 1/8 teaspoon ground cloves, or a combination of your choice. Recommended coatings: Gingerbread, Basic.

45

Flavoring Marshmallows with Juices and Other Liquids

It's a simple matter to flavor marshmallows with juice, liqueurs, or wine. In fact, some fruits translate much better in their juice form because their textures might be too grainy for good marshmallow consistency. You'll find a variety of ways to use liquid flavorings in this chapter; some juices are used just as they are, some are reduced to enhance their flavors, and others are used in frozen concentrate form. Wines, liqueurs, champagne, and even tequila or brandy can be used to interesting effect. Be sure to use unsweetened juices so the balance of sugar in the recipe isn't affected.

Apple Marshmallows

You can do all kinds of things with apple marshmallows. The flavor works with caramel, spices, and sweet potatoes. I used juice to make them because the grainy texture of apples interferes with the smooth texture of the marshmallow. To get a full apple flavor, you need to use apple juice concentrate rather than apple juice. The recipe uses a full 12-ounce can.

For the bloom:

4 tablespoons unflavored gelatin

3/4 cup thawed apple juice concentrate at cool room temperature

1/3 cup cold water

For the base:

3/4 cup thawed apple juice concentrate

1/2 cup water

3/4 cup Marshmallow Syrup (page 26)

Pinch salt

1 1/2 cups granulated cane sugar

Prepare a pan by coating it with nonstick spray, then wiping it lightly with a paper towel so that only a thin film of oil remains.

Make the bloom. Place the gelatin in a bowl and whisk in the apple juice concentrate and cold water until there are no lumps. Set the bowl near the stove.

Place the ingredients for the base in a heavy 4-quart saucepan over medium-high heat, and stir until all of the sugar is moistened. Bring the mixture to a boil and cover the pan, boiling for 2 minutes. Then remove the cover, insert a candy thermometer, and cook the base to 250 degrees F. *Do not stir the mixture once the lid has been removed.* Turn off the heat and gently stir the bloomed gelatin into the base. Pour the batter into the bowl of a stand mixer. Gradually increase the mixer speed to high and beat the batter for 11 minutes. You can cover the mixer with a clean kitchen towel for the first 3 or 4 minutes to avoid splattering hot liquid on yourself.

Spread the marshmallow batter into the prepared pan and let it set, uncovered, for 4 hours, or overnight. Cut and coat as desired. Once cut, the marshmallows will keep for 7 to 10 days in an airtight container with a corner slightly ajar. Recommended coatings: Basic, Gingerbread, Cinnamon, chopped nuts.

Orange Marshmallows

Looking for a refreshing treat after school or as a lunch dessert? This is one your kids will love. It delivers a big orange punch and a bright flavor. You can also serve it cubed in fruit salad, with vanilla ice cream, or in small chunks in a mango salsa. It's a pretty yellow color with vibrant orange flecks.

For the bloom:

1/2 cup frozen orange juice concentrate, thawed

1/2 cup strained freshly squeezed orange juice, or no-pulp purchased orange juice

3 tablespoons unflavored gelatin

For the base:

1/2 cup water

1 1/4 cups Marshmallow Syrup (page 26)

1 1/2 cups granulated cane sugar

Pinch salt

Additional flavoring:

1 to 2 tablespoons freshly grated orange zest

Prepare a pan by coating it with nonstick spray, then wiping it lightly with a paper towel so that only a thin film of oil remains.

Make the bloom. In a small bowl, whisk the orange juice concentrate and the orange juice into the gelatin until there are no lumps. Set the bowl near the stove.

Place the base ingredients into a heavy 4-quart saucepan set over medium-high heat, and stir to moisten the sugar. Bring the base to a boil and cover the pan. Boil for 2 minutes, remove the lid, and insert a candy thermometer. Cook the base to 255 degrees F. Do not stir the mixture once the lid has been removed. Turn off the heat, remove the thermometer, and add the bloomed gelatin to the pan, stirring gently.

Pour the batter into the bowl of a stand mixer and gradually increase the speed to high. Beat for 10 minutes, covering the mixer with a clean kitchen towel for the first 3 or 4 minutes to avoid splattering hot liquid on yourself. Remove the bowl from the stand and fold in the orange zest.

Spread the batter into the prepared pan, smooth the top, and let it cure, uncovered, for at least 4 hours or overnight. Cut and coat the marshmallows as desired, and store them in an airtight container, with one corner slightly ajar, for up to 2 weeks at room temperature. Recommended coatings: Fruit Powder, Basic, ground or shaved chocolate, coconut.

Lemon Marshmallows

Lemon is one of my favorite flavors. It's bright, fresh, and versatile. Lemon Marshmallows make wonderful spring treats, cut into fancy shapes and sprinkled with colored sugars, or piped into mounds and coated with chocolate.

For the bloom:

3 tablespoons unflavored gelatin

²/₃ cup strained freshly squeezed lemon juice

For the base:

¹/₄ cup water

¹/₂ cup strained freshly squeezed lemon juice

1 cup Marshmallow Syrup (page 26)

Pinch salt

1 ¹/₂ cups granulated cane sugar

Additional flavoring:

1 tablespoon minced freshly grated lemon zest

Prepare a pan by coating it with nonstick spray, then wiping it lightly with a paper towel so that only a thin film of oil remains.

Make the bloom. Place the gelatin in a small bowl and whisk in the lemon juice until smooth. Set the bowl near the stove.

Put the base ingredients into a 4-quart saucepan set over medium-high heat, stirring gently to moisten the sugar. Bring the base to a boil, cover the pan, and boil for 2 minutes. Remove the cover, insert a candy thermometer, and cook the base until it reaches 240 degrees F. *Do not stir the mixture once the lid has been removed.* Turn off the heat, remove the thermometer, and gently stir the bloomed gelatin into the cooked base.

Pour the batter into the bowl of a stand mixer and gradually increase the speed to high, beating for 12 minutes. You can cover the mixer with a clean kitchen towel for the first 3 or 4 minutes to avoid splattering hot liquid on yourself. Remove the bowl from the stand and fold in the zest.

Spread the marshmallow batter into the prepared pan, smoothing the top, and let it cure, uncovered, for at least 4 hours or overnight. Cut and coat as desired. Store the cut marshmallows in an airtight container, with a corner slightly ajar, for up to 2 weeks. Recommended coatings: Citrus, Basic, shredded coconut, tempered chocolate.

Mango Marshmallows

Mango is one of the tropical fruits that can't be used raw, so an easy way around that is to use 100 percent mango nectar or juice to make marshmallows. It's not easy to find, but it's worth it when you do. Mix chunks of these marshmallows into fruit salad or serve them with grilled meats.

For the bloom:

3 tablespoons unflavored gelatin

1 1/2 cups 100 percent mango juice or nectar

For the base:

1 cup 100 percent mango nectar or juice

1 1/4 cups Marshmallow Syrup (page 26)

Pinch salt

1 3/4 cups granulated cane sugar

Prepare a pan by coating it with nonstick spray, then wiping it lightly with a paper towel so that only a thin film of oil remains.

Make the bloom. Place the gelatin in a small bowl and whisk in the mango juice until smooth. Set the bowl near the stove.

Place all of the base ingredients into a heavy 4-quart saucepan over medium-high heat, stirring to moisten all of the sugar. Bring the mixture to a boil, cover the pan, and boil for 2 minutes. Remove the cover, insert a candy thermometer, and cook the base to 250 degrees F. *Do not stir the mixture once the lid has been removed.* Turn off the heat, remove the thermometer, and gently stir in the bloom.

Pour the batter into the bowl of a stand mixer and gradually increase the speed to high, beating the mixture for 10 minutes. You can cover the mixer with a clean kitchen towel for the first 3 or 4 minutes to avoid splattering hot liquid on yourself. Spread the batter into the prepared pan. Let the marshmallow cure, uncovered, for at least 4 hours or overnight. Cut and coat as desired. Store the marshmallows in an airtight container, with a corner slightly ajar, for up to 1 week. Recommended coatings: Fruit Powder, shredded coconut.

Toasted Coconut Marshmallows

Serve these sweet treats with an assortment of other tropical fruit–flavored marshmallows for a light picnic dessert. Mango, Passion Fruit, and Orange marshmallows would make a lovely group. Orange spritzers round out the experience. Be careful to use coconut milk in the marshmallows and not coconut cream, which contains significantly different ingredients.

   Also, it's important that you use "lite" coconut milk, which has $1/3$ to $1/4$ of the fat that you will find in regular coconut milk. The marshmallow batter cannot support all of that fat.

For the bloom:

4 tablespoons gelatin

$2/3$ cup "lite" coconut milk

For the base:

$1/2$ cup + 2 tablespoons water

$1 1/2$ cups Marshmallow Syrup (page 26)

2 cups granulated cane sugar

Pinch salt

Additional flavoring:

$1/4$ cup "lite" coconut milk

For the coating:

2 cups coconut

Prepare a pan by coating it with nonstick spray, then wiping it lightly with a paper towel so that only a thin film of oil remains.

First make the bloom. Place the gelatin in a small bowl and stir in the coconut milk until there are no lumps. Set the bowl near the stove.

Place the base ingredients in a heavy 4-quart saucepan over medium heat. Bring the mixture to a boil, cover the pan, and boil for 2 minutes. Remove the cover, insert a candy thermometer, and cook the base to 260 degrees F. *Do not stir the mixture once the lid has been removed.* When the base reaches 260 degrees F, turn off the heat, remove the thermometer, and stir in the bloomed gelatin.

Pour the batter into the bowl of a stand mixer and gradually increase the speed to high. Cover the mixer with a clean kitchen towel for the first 3 or 4 minutes to avoid splattering hot liquid on yourself. Beat the batter for a total of 12 minutes.

When there is just 1 minute of beating time left, very slowly drizzle in the "lite" coconut milk. Then continue beating for another 30 seconds. Scrape the mixture into the prepared pan and let it cure, uncovered, for at least 4 hours or overnight.

Preheat an oven to 325 degrees F and spread the coconut evenly in 1 layer on a baking sheet. Bake in the preheated oven for 20 to 30 minutes, stirring often. Cut the marshmallows as desired, and coat them with the toasted coconut. Store them in an airtight container, with a corner slightly ajar, for up to 2 weeks. Recommended coatings: Cocoa, Fruit Powder, chocolate shavings, tempered chocolate.

Honey Pear Marshmallows

The flavors of pear and honey complement each other well in these delightful marshmallows. The color is a lovely pearl white. Serve them with tea or float them in hot cider. To get a full pear flavor, the nectar must be reduced and cooled before you make the marshmallows, so allow time for this.

For the reduced pear nectar:

6 cups 100 percent pear juice or pear nectar

For the bloom:

3 1/2 tablespoons unflavored gelatin

1 cup cooled reduced pear nectar or juice at cool room temperature

For the base:

1 cup reduced pear juice or nectar

1/3 cup mild-flavored honey

3/4 cup Marshmallow Syrup (page 26)

Pinch salt

1 1/2 cups granulated cane sugar

Pour the 6 cups of pear nectar into a 4-quart saucepan over medium-high heat and reduce it to 2 cups, skimming off any foam that forms on the surface. Set it aside to cool to room temperature.

Prepare a pan by coating it with nonstick spray, then wiping it lightly with a paper towel so that only a thin film of oil remains.

Make the bloom. Place the gelatin in a small bowl. Pour 1 cup of reduced pear nectar over the gelatin, stirring with a small whisk or fork until it is free of any lumps. Set the bowl near the stove.

Put all of the base ingredients into a heavy 4-quart saucepan over medium-high heat, stirring gently with a heatproof spatula until the sugar has all been moistened. Bring the mixture to a boil, cover the pan, and boil for 2 minutes. Remove the lid, insert a thermometer, and boil the base until it reaches 250 degrees F. *Do not stir the mixture once the lid has been removed.* Turn off the heat, remove the thermometer, and add the bloomed gelatin, stirring gently with a heatproof spatula.

Pour the base into the bowl of a stand mixer, and slowly turn up the mixer speed to high, beating for 10 minutes. You can cover the mixer with a clean kitchen towel for the first 3 or 4 minutes to avoid splattering hot liquid on yourself.

Spread the batter into the prepared pan and smooth the top with a lightly oiled spatula or with a wet hand. Let the marshmallow cure in the pan for at least 4 hours or overnight. After cutting the batter into marshmallows, store them in a container, with a corner slightly ajar, for up to 2 weeks. Recommended coatings: Basic, Vanilla, Cinnamon, Fruit Powder.

Key Lime Marshmallows

This is for my friend Annie, who told me that I had to have a recipe for Key Lime Marshmallows in this book. More tart than standard Persian limes, and with a striking bitterness to the juice, key limes can be found most often between May and September in the United States. They range in size from 1 to 2 inches in diameter. Freshly squeezed key lime juice is far superior to the bottled version. The skins are unusually thin, so use as little pressure as possible when grating the limes to avoid the very bitter white pith.

For the bloom:

3 tablespoons unflavored
  gelatin

3/4 cup strained freshly
  squeezed key lime juice

For the base:

1/2 cup water

1 1/4 cups Marshmallow
  Syrup (page 26)

Pinch salt

1 3/4 cups granulated
  cane sugar

Additional flavoring:

1 teaspoon freshly grated
  key lime zest

Prepare a pan by coating it with nonstick spray, then wiping it lightly with a paper towel so that only a thin film of oil remains.

Make the bloom. Put the gelatin in a small bowl and whisk in the key lime juice until smooth. Place the bowl near the stove.

Put the base ingredients into a heavy 4-quart saucepan set over medium-high heat and bring the base to a boil. Cover and boil the mixture for 2 minutes. Remove the cover, insert a thermometer, and cook the base to 240 degrees F. *Do not stir the mixture once the lid has been removed.* Turn off the heat, remove the thermometer, and gently stir the bloomed gelatin into the base.

Pour the batter into the bowl of a stand mixer. Gradually increase the mixer speed to high and beat the mixture for 12 minutes. You can cover the mixer with a clean kitchen towel for the first 3 or 4 minutes to avoid splattering hot liquid on yourself.

Remove the bowl from the stand and fold in the zest. Spread the marshmallow batter into the prepared pan and let it cure, uncovered, for at least 4 hours or overnight. Cut and coat as desired, and store the marshmallows in an airtight container, with a corner of the lid slightly ajar, for a week. Recommended coatings: Citrus, Basic, shredded coconut.

Margarita Marshmallows

Once it's warm enough to sit out on our terrace at night, we like to begin the weekend with margaritas on Friday evenings. As I was drinking one during the development of recipes for this book, I found myself wondering how to turn it into a marshmallow. It's a sweet way to have your margarita and eat it too!

For the bloom:

3 ½ tablespoons unflavored gelatin

⅓ cup tequila

⅓ cup strained freshly squeezed, or no-pulp store-bought, orange juice

⅓ cup strained freshly squeezed lime juice

For the base:

½ cup tequila

1 ½ cups Marshmallow Syrup (page 26)

1 ½ cups granulated cane sugar

¼ teaspoon salt

Prepare a pan by coating it with nonstick spray, then wiping it lightly with a paper towel so that only a thin film of oil remains.

Make the bloom. Place the gelatin in a small bowl and stir in the tequila and juices with a fork or small whisk until there are no lumps. Set the bowl near the stove.

Place all of the base ingredients into a heavy 4-quart saucepan set over medium-high heat and stir to moisten all of the sugar. Bring the mixture to a boil, cover the pan, and continue boiling for 2 minutes. Remove the cover, insert a candy thermometer, and cook the base until it reaches 240 degrees F. *Do not stir the mixture once the lid has been removed.* Turn off the heat, remove the thermometer, and gently stir in the bloomed gelatin.

Pour the batter into the bowl of a stand mixer. Gradually increase the speed to high and beat for 10 minutes, covering the mixer with a clean kitchen towel for the first 3 or 4 minutes to avoid splattering hot liquid on yourself.

Spread the marshmallow batter into the prepared pan and let it cure for at least 4 hours or overnight. Cut and coat as desired, and store the marshmallows in an airtight container, with a corner of the lid slightly ajar, for a week. Recommended coatings: Citrus, Basic.

Peach Marshmallows

Full of the flavor and aroma of freshly made peach pie filling, these marshmallows taste like a summer afternoon. If you don't have fresh local peaches that are ripe and sweet, be sure to use sliced peaches frozen without sugar. The marshmallows will only have as much flavor as the peaches you use to make them. For an easy dessert, serve them on a plate with shortbread cookies or vanilla wafers. It will taste just like a peach chiffon pie.

For the bloom:

3 tablespoons unflavored gelatin

1 1/4 cups peeled, sliced, and pureed peaches (10 ounces fresh, peeled and pitted or thawed frozen peaches)

For the base:

1 1/3 cups 100 percent peach juice or nectar

1 1/4 cups Marshmallow Syrup (page 26)

Pinch salt

1 3/4 cups granulated cane sugar

Prepare a pan by coating it with nonstick spray, then wiping it lightly with a paper towel so that only a thin film of oil remains.

Make the bloom. Place the gelatin in a bowl and whisk in the peach puree until smooth. Set the bowl near the stove.

Place the base ingredients in a heavy 4-quart saucepan and stir to moisten the sugar. Bring the base to a boil over medium heat, cover the pan, and boil for 2 minutes. Remove the cover, insert a thermometer, and increase the heat to medium high. *Do not stir the mixture once the lid has been removed.* Cook the base to 250 degrees F. Turn off the heat, remove the thermometer, and gently stir in the bloomed gelatin.

Pour the batter into the bowl of a stand mixer and beat the mixture on high speed for 10 minutes. Scrape the marshmallow batter into the prepared pan, smoothing the top, and let it cure for 4 hours or overnight. Cut and coat the marshmallows as desired, and store in a covered container, with a corner of the lid slightly ajar, for up to 2 weeks. Recommended coatings: Basic, Fruit Powder.

Champagne Marshmallows

Nothing seems so extravagant or so luxurious as champagne marshmallows. Try this with a dry champagne, Spanish cava, or Italian prosecco. It's a good way to use up any leftover bubbly you might have on hand. If you're feeling over-the-edge indulgent, coat the cut marshmallows in ground semisweet chocolate or dip them in tempered chocolate. (For instructions on tempering chocolate, see page 147.)

For the bloom:

3 tablespoons unflavored
gelatin

²/₃ cup cold, flat
sparkling wine

1 ½ teaspoons vanilla
paste

For the base:

½ cup flat sparkling
wine

1 cup Marshmallow
Syrup (page 26)

Pinch salt

1 ½ cups granulated
cane sugar

Prepare a pan by coating it with nonstick spray, then wiping it lightly with a paper towel so that only a thin film of oil remains.

Make the bloom. Place the gelatin in a bowl, add the sparkling wine and vanilla paste, and whisk until completely smooth. Set the bloom near the stove.

Place all of the base ingredients into a heavy 4-quart saucepan set over medium-high heat, stirring gently to moisten all of the sugar. Bring the base to a boil and cover the pan, boiling for 2 minutes. Remove the cover, insert a candy thermometer, and continue cooking until the base reaches 250 degrees F. *Do not stir the mixture once the lid has been removed.* Turn off the heat, remove the thermometer, and gently stir in the bloom.

Pour the batter into the bowl of a stand mixer and gradually increase the speed to high, beating for 9 minutes. You can cover the mixer with a clean kitchen towel for the first 3 or 4 minutes to avoid splattering hot liquid on yourself.

Spread the marshmallow batter into the prepared pan and let it cure, uncovered, for at least 4 hours or overnight. Cut and coat as desired. Recommended coatings: Basic, Cocoa, Long Pepper, ground chocolate.

Amaretto Marshmallows

The mellow flavor of Amaretto works especially well in marshmallows. Serve them with coffee after dinner, or coat them with chocolate and give them as gifts at the holidays. You can also make these marshmallows substituting Frangelica or Grand Marnier for the Amaretto.

For the bloom:

3 tablespoons unflavored gelatin

²/₃ cup Amaretto

For the base:

¹/₂ cup water

*1 cup Marshmallow Syrup
(page 26)*

Pinch salt

1 ¹/₂ cups granulated cane sugar

Prepare a pan by coating it with nonstick spray, then wiping it lightly with a paper towel so that only a thin film of oil remains.

Make the bloom. Place the gelatin in a bowl and add the Amaretto, whisking until completely smooth. Set the bloom near the stove.

Place all of the base ingredients into a heavy 4-quart saucepan set over medium-high heat, stirring gently to moisten all of the sugar. Bring the base to a boil and cover the pan, boiling for 2 minutes. Remove the cover, insert a candy thermometer, and continue cooking until the base reaches 250 degrees F. *Do not stir the mixture once the lid has been removed*. Turn off the heat, remove the thermometer, and gently stir in the bloom.

Pour the batter into the bowl of a stand mixer and gradually increase the speed to high, beating for 9 minutes. You can cover the mixer with a clean kitchen towel for the first 3 or 4 minutes to avoid splattering hot liquid on yourself.

Spread the marshmallow batter into the prepared pan and let it cure, uncovered, for at least 4 hours or overnight. Cut and coat as desired. Recommended coatings: Basic, Vanilla, Cinnamon, finely chopped almonds, chocolate shavings, tempered chocolate.

Limoncello Marshmallows

Anyone who has been to Italy knows the captivating attraction of limoncello, a liqueur made from lemons. It is served throughout Italy, and many families have made their own version, passing the recipe down from one generation to another. It's especially popular along the Amalfi coast, south of Rome. Most limoncellos are made using only the rind, and not the juice of the lemon, and they are delicious, but sweet. Look for a brand such as Caravella Limoncello that also uses the juice; it has a tart aspect that works well in marshmallows.

Prepare Amaretto Marshmallows according to the recipe, replacing the Amaretto with limoncello.

Infusing Marshmallows with Spices and Herbs

Spices and herbs play such an enormous role throughout the world that it would be a shame not to infuse them into marshmallows. When spices are infused rather than added ground, the flavors are rounder and subtler. Herbs also take on a dreamy role when they are infused. You'll find ways to infuse both spices and herbs in this section, and I hope you'll try making up some of your own combinations.

Cinnamon Mocha Marshmallows.

Apple Spice Marshmallows

Apples and spice are a combination that evokes memories of the fall: Halloween, football games, falling leaves, and crisp, cold air. Infusing the spices in this recipe gives a warm flavor to the marshmallows without being harsh. Try using your own selection of spices to satisfy your tastes. Calvados, an apple liqueur, heightens the flavors in this marshmallow.

For the bloom:

4 tablespoons unflavored gelatin

2 tablespoons Calvados

³/₄ cup thawed apple juice concentrate

¹/₃ cup cold water

For the base:

¹/₄ cup thawed apple juice concentrate

¹/₂ cup water

³/₄ cup Marshmallow Syrup (page 26)

Pinch salt

1 ¹/₂ cups granulated cane sugar

Additional flavoring (placed in a tea ball):

2 whole cloves

5 whole allspice, lightly crushed

Three 3-inch sticks cinnamon, lightly crushed

1 teaspoon black peppercorns, lightly crushed

Prepare a pan by coating it with nonstick spray, then wiping it lightly with a paper towel so that only a thin film of oil remains.

Make the bloom. Place the gelatin in a bowl and whisk in the Calvados, apple juice concentrate, and cold water until there are no lumps. Set the bowl near the stove.

Place the base ingredients in a heavy 4-quart saucepan over medium-high heat, and stir until all of the sugar is moistened. Bring the mixture to a boil and put the tea ball into the pan, making sure the spices are submerged. Cover the pan and remove it from the heat, allowing the spices to infuse for 30 minutes. Bring the base back to a boil and cover the pan, boiling for 2 minutes. Then remove the cover, insert a candy thermometer, and cook the base to 250 degrees F. *Do not stir the mixture once the lid has been removed.* Turn off the heat, remove the thermometer and tea ball, and gently stir the bloomed gelatin into the base.

Pour the batter into the bowl of a stand mixer, gradually increasing the mixer speed to high, and beat it for 11 minutes. You can cover the mixer with a clean kitchen towel for the first 3 or 4 minutes to avoid splattering hot liquid on yourself.

Spread the marshmallow batter into the prepared pan and let it set, uncovered, for 4 hours or overnight. Cut and coat as desired. Once cut, the marshmallows will keep for 7 to 10 days. Recommended coatings: Basic, Cinnamon, Gingerbread.

Cinnamon Mocha Marshmallows

Mildly flavored with cocoa and scented with cinnamon, these subtle marshmallows will surprise you with their allure. They are irresistible with a cup of authentic hot chocolate. Use the best cocoa you can afford.

For the cocoa slurry:

1/2 cup natural unsweetened cocoa

2 teaspoons instant espresso crystals or powder

1/2 cup boiling water

For the base:

1/2 cup water

1 1/4 cups Marshmallow Syrup (page 26)

Pinch salt

1 1/2 cups granulated cane sugar

Three 3-inch sticks cinnamon, lightly crushed, in a tea ball

For the bloom:

4 tablespoons unflavored gelatin

1/2 cup cold water

2 teaspoons pure vanilla extract

Prepare a pan by coating it with nonstick spray, then wiping it lightly with a paper towel so that only a thin film of oil remains.

First make the cocoa slurry. Place the cocoa and espresso powder in a small bowl. Add the boiling water, stirring with a small whisk until perfectly smooth. Set near the stove.

Place all of the ingredients for the base except the tea ball into a heavy 4-quart saucepan over medium heat, stirring with a heatproof spatula until the sugar is moistened. When the mixture comes to a boil, cover the pan, turn off the heat, and allow the cinnamon to steep for 30 minutes. Bring the base back to a boil, covered, for 2 minutes. Uncover the pan, insert a candy thermometer and the tea ball, making sure the cinnamon is submerged in the base, and cook the base until it reaches 260 degrees F. *Do not stir the mixture once the lid has been removed.*

While the base is cooking, make the bloom. Place the gelatin in a small bowl. Add the water and vanilla extract and stir with a small whisk until the mixture is perfectly smooth. Set near the stove.

Once the temperature of the base reaches 260 degrees F, turn off the heat, remove the thermometer and the tea ball, and add the bloomed gelatin and the cocoa slurry, stirring gently with a heatproof spatula. The mixture will boil up quite high. Pour the batter into the bowl of a stand mixer, gradually bring the speed to high, being careful of hot splatters, and beat for 18 minutes. This batter splatters considerably at the beginning of the beating stage; you can throw a kitchen towel over the mixture for the first 5 minutes to avoid splatters.

Spread the batter into the prepared pan, and smooth the top. Let the pan sit at room temperature for at least 4 hours or overnight, before cutting and coating. Cover the pan loosely with an oiled piece of foil while the marshmallows cure. Store the marshmallows in an airtight container, with a corner slightly ajar, for up to 2 weeks. Recommended coatings: Cocoa, Cinnamon, chocolate shavings, ground chocolate, tempered chocolate.

Sauvignon Blanc– Long Pepper Marshmallows

Long pepper is an Asian spice related to black peppercorns that resembles inch-long, very slender closed pinecones. It is available in some specialty stores and online (see resources, page 173).

For the bloom:

3 tablespoons unflavored
    gelatin

$2/3$ cup sauvignon blanc

$1^1/_2$ teaspoons vanilla paste

For the base:

$1/_2$ cup sauvignon blanc

1 cup Marshmallow Syrup
    (page 26)

Pinch salt

$1^1/_2$ cups granulated cane
    sugar

1 tablespoon crushed long
    pepper, in a tea ball

Prepare a pan by coating it with nonstick spray, then wiping it lightly with a paper towel so that only a thin film of oil remains.

Make the bloom. Place the gelatin in a bowl. Add the sauvignon blanc and vanilla paste, whisking until completely smooth. Set the bloom near the stove.

Make the base. Place the first 4 ingredients into a heavy 4-quart saucepan set over medium-high heat, stirring gently to moisten the sugar. When the base comes to a boil, place the tea ball with long pepper in the pan so the it is submerged. Cover the pan, turn off the heat, and let it infuse for 30 minutes. Bring the base back to a boil, covered, for 2 minutes. Remove the cover, insert a candy thermometer, and cook the base to 250 degrees F. *Do not stir the mixture once the lid has been removed.*

Remove the thermometer and the tea ball and gently stir in the bloom. Pour the batter into the bowl of a stand mixer and gradually increase the speed to high, beating for 11 minutes. You can cover the mixer with a clean kitchen towel to avoid splattering hot liquid on yourself.

Spread the marshmallow batter into the prepared pan and let it cure, uncovered, for at least 4 hours or overnight. Cut and coat as desired. Recommended coatings: Basic, Long Pepper, Cocoa, chocolate shavings, ground chocolate.

Lemon, Honey, and Cardamom Marshmallows

Cardamom is an aromatic and pleasantly unusually flavored spice. It's best to buy it in pod form, but if that's not available, buy the seeds for this recipe. The seeds are removed from the pods, and dry-toasting them in a hot skillet enhances the flavor.

For the bloom:

3 tablespoons unflavored gelatin

2/3 cup strained freshly squeezed lemon juice

For the base:

2 tablespoons cardamom seeds (removed from the pods)

1/4 cup water

1/2 cup strained freshly squeezed lemon juice

1 cup honey

Pinch salt

1 1/2 cups granulated cane sugar

Additional flavoring:

1 tablespoon minced freshly grated lemon zest

Prepare a pan by coating it with nonstick spray, then wiping it lightly with a paper towel so that only a thin film of oil remains.

Make the bloom. Place the gelatin in a small bowl and whisk in the lemon juice until smooth. Set the bowl near the stove.

Heat a heavy skillet over medium-high heat and toast the cardamom seeds for a minute or 2. Lightly crush them and put them into a tea ball.

Place the remaining base ingredients into a 4-quart saucepan set over medium-high heat, stirring gently to moisten the sugar. Bring the base to a boil and put the tea ball into the base, immersing the cardamom seeds. Turn off the heat. cover the pan and let the spice steep in the base for 30 minutes.

Bring the base back to a boil. Cover the pan and boil for 2 minutes. Remove the cover, insert a candy thermometer, and cook the base until it reaches 240 degrees F. *Do not stir the mixture once the lid has been removed.* Remove the tea ball and thermometer and gently stir the bloomed gelatin into the cooked base.

Pour the batter into the bowl of a stand mixer and gradually increase the speed to high, beating for 12 minutes. You can cover the mixer with a clean kitchen towel to avoid splattering hot liquid on yourself. Remove the bowl from the stand and fold in the zest. Recommended coating: Basic.

Honey-Lavender Marshmallows

The combination of honey and lavender is fragrant and sensuous. Use a mild-flavored honey so the lavender isn't overwhelmed. These are perfect marshmallows to serve with tea or to package in pretty bags tied with ribbons to give as gifts. Attach a fresh edible flower to the tops of the marshmallows with a bit of marshmallow syrup and take a plate of them as a hostess gift. Everyone will marvel at you.

For the bloom:

3 tablespoons unflavored gelatin

1/2 cup + 2 tablespoons cold water

For the base:

3/4 cup water

1 1/4 cups honey

Pinch salt

1 1/2 cups granulated cane sugar

2 to 3 tablespoons lavender, in a tea ball

Prepare a pan by coating it with nonstick spray, then wiping it lightly with a paper towel so that only a thin film of oil remains.

Make the bloom. Place the gelatin into a small bowl and whisk in the water until there are no lumps. Set the bowl near the stove.

Make the base. Place the water, honey, salt, and sugar, in that order, into a 6-quart pan. Bring the mixture to a boil over medium-high heat, put the tea ball in the pan so that the lavender is immersed in the base, and turn off the heat. Cover the pan and let the lavender steep for 30 minutes. Bring the base back to a boil, covered, for 2 minutes. Remove the lid, insert a candy thermometer, and continue boiling until the thermometer reaches 250 degrees F. *Do not stir the mixture once the lid has been removed.* Remove the thermometer and tea ball and gently stir in the bloomed gelatin.

Pour the batter into the bowl of an electric stand mixer, gradually increasing to high speed, and beat for 10 to 12 minutes. You can cover the mixer with a clean kitchen towel for the first 3 or 4 minutes to avoid splattering hot liquid on yourself.

Spread the marshmallow batter into the prepared pan, smoothing the top. Let the pan sit out at room temperature, uncovered, for at least 4 hours or overnight. Cut and coat as desired. The marshmallows will keep for up to 2 weeks at room temperature. Recommended coating: Basic.

Flavoring Marshmallows in Additional Ways

By now you have probably figured out that there is more to marshmallows than just vanilla. This section deals with ways to flavor marshmallows that aren't dealt with in the previous sections. Since they rely on air for a large part of their texture and identity, the most difficult flavoring agents to use are the ones that contain fat because the air pockets in the marshmallows can't easily support it. It requires folding the heavy culprit into the marshmallow batter at the end of the process. This section also includes recipes that are easily made but require just a little extra attention so the flavors come through. Follow the instructions and you'll be rewarded with great taste and unusual flavors that will truly wow your family and friends.

Chocolate Marshmallow.

Chocolate Marshmallows

MAKES A 7 X 11 X 1-INCH PAN   (See photo, page 72.)

Lusciously flavored with chocolate and cocoa, these creamy marshmallows are a delight for chocolate lovers and kids alike, and are irresistible eaten out of hand. Use a natural unsweetened cocoa that contains 1 to 1.5 grams of fat per tablespoon (look at the nutrition label for this information). If you use cocoa with more fat, you could be left with heavy marshmallows instead of fluffy ones, and they will lose their luscious flavor and texture. I use boiling water in the slurry because it heightens the flavor of the cocoa. Buy the best dark chocolate you can for this recipe, and use the highest-quality, darkest-color cocoa you can find for the coating mixture. Penzeys Spices carries a good, dark cocoa, as does King Arthur (see resources, page 173).

For the cocoa slurry:

1/2 cup natural unsweetened cocoa (see note above)

1 tablespoon instant espresso crystals or powder

2/3 cup boiling water

For the base:

1/2 cup water

1 1/4 cups Marshmallow Syrup (page 26)

Pinch salt

1 1/2 cups granulated cane sugar

For the bloom:

4 tablespoons unflavored gelatin

1/2 cup cold water

2 teaspoons pure vanilla extract

Additional flavoring:

2 ounces fine quality semisweet chocolate (54 percent cocoa solids or higher)

Prepare a pan by coating it with nonstick spray, then wiping it lightly with a paper towel so that only a thin film of oil remains.

First, make the cocoa slurry. Place the cocoa and espresso powder in a small bowl. Add the boiling water, stirring with a small whisk until perfectly smooth. Set near the stove.

Next, make the base. Place all the ingredients for the base into a heavy 4-quart saucepan over medium heat, stirring with a heatproof spatula until all the sugar is moistened. When the mixture comes to a boil, cover and boil the base for 2 minutes. Remove the lid, insert a candy thermometer, increase to medium high, and boil the mixture until it reaches 260 degrees F. *Do not stir the mixture once the lid has been removed.*

While the base is cooking, make the bloom. Place the gelatin in a small bowl. Measure the water and add the vanilla extract to it. Pour the water mixture into the gelatin, stirring with a small whisk until the mixture is perfectly smooth. Set near the stove.

Once the temperature of the base reaches 260 degrees F, turn off the heat, remove the thermome-ter, and add the bloomed gelatin, stirring gently with a heatproof spatula. The mixture will boil up. Add the cocoa slurry and gently stir again. Pour the batter into the bowl of a stand mixer, gradually bring the speed to high, being careful of hot splatters, and beat for 18 minutes. This batter seriously splatters at the beginning of the beating stage; you can throw a kitchen towel over the mixture for the first 5 minutes to avoid splatters. When there are 5 minutes remaining, melt the chocolate and place a medium-size bowl and spatula near the mixer.

When the batter has finished beating, remove the bowl from the mixer, scoop about 1 1/2 cups of batter into the medium bowl, and fold the melted chocolate into it. Fold this mixture back into the batter as evenly as possible, spread it into the pre-pared pan, and smooth the top. Let the pan sit at room temperature for at least 4 hours or overnight. Cover the pan loosely with an oiled piece of foil while the marshmallows cure. Cut and coat as desired. Store the marshmallows in an airtight container, with a corner slightly ajar, for up to 2 weeks. Recommended coatings: Cocoa, Vanilla, Long Pepper, coconut, shaved chocolate, tem-pered chocolate.

Chocolate-Malted Marshmallows

Make Chocolate Marshmallows (page 74), using only 1 1/2 teaspoons of vanilla, omitting the espresso powder, and adding 3/4 cup Malt Flavor Ovaltine to the cocoa slurry. Cover the pan loosely with an oiled piece of foil while the marshmallows cure. Recommended coating: Cocoa, Vanilla, Fruit Powder, shaved chocolate, tempered chocolate.

Chocolate-Peppermint Marshmallows

My daughter and I could have eaten the entire bowl of this marshmallow batter before it even made it into the pan to cure. Use a high-quality peppermint flavor, *not extract,* to get the best results. My favorite brand is Boyajian Natural Peppermint Flavor because it has a great taste without any harshness (see resources, page 173). If you use another brand you may need a little more or a little less, depending on the strength of the flavor.

Make the Chocolate Marshmallows (page 74) according to the recipe, omitting the espresso powder and vanilla extract and adding 1 1/4 teaspoons pure peppermint flavor to the bloom. Cover the pan loosely with an oiled piece of foil while the marshmallows cure. Recommended coating: Cocoa.

Chocolate-Ancho Chile Marshmallows

Sweet and seductive with a warm finish, the combination of chocolate and ancho chile is one of my favorites. It nurtures the child in us while feeding our adult passions. Ancho chiles provide a warm heat that sneaks up at the end.

Make Chocolate Marshmallows (page 74), adding 2 teaspoons ancho chile powder to the cocoa slurry.

Caramel Marshmallows

Many people confuse caramel with butterscotch, but they are two different things. Caramel has a more sophisticated flavor. Make sure you don't let the sugar get too dark, or your marshmallows will have a bitter flavor.

For the caramel:

2 cups granulated cane sugar

½ cup water

½ teaspoon lemon juice

For the base:

½ cup hot water

1 cup Marshmallow Syrup (page 26)

Pinch salt

For the bloom:

3 tablespoons unflavored gelatin

¾ cup water

½ teaspoon pure vanilla extract

Additional flavoring:

1 tablespoon butter (European style
    will taste better here), cut into
    3 or 4 pieces

Prepare a pan by coating it with nonstick spray, then wiping it lightly with a paper towel so that only a thin film of oil remains.

Stir all ingredients for the caramel in a heavy 4-quart saucepan set over medium heat; wash down any crystals of sugar that are on the sides of the pan with a pastry brush that has been dipped in water. *Do not stir the caramel after you have washed down the sides of the pan.* Cook the mixture, watching it carefully, for about 8 to 15 minutes, or until it turns a medium amber color. It will continue to cook after it has been removed from the heat.

Remove the pan from the heat and carefully add the base ingredients, stirring to combine. Any thick caramel will dissolve as the base cooks. Bring the base to a boil over medium-high heat, again washing down any sugar crystals from the sides of the pan. Insert a candy thermometer and cook the base to 250 degrees F.

While the base is cooking, make the bloom. Place the gelatin in a small bowl. Measure the water and vanilla extract to it. Pour the water mixture into the gelatin, stirring with a small whisk until the mixture is perfectly smooth.

Add the bloom to the base, stirring gently, and pour the batter into the bowl of a stand mixer. Gradually increase the speed of the mixer to high. You can cover the mixer with a clean kitchen towel for the first 3 or 4 minutes to avoid splattering hot liquid on yourself. Beat the batter for 10 minutes.

While the batter is beating, melt the butter slowly so that there are still a couple of lumps, remove it from the heat, and stir with a whisk so it is creamy and thick. If the butter separates, you must start again with new butter.

Remove the bowl from the stand and fold the butter carefully into the batter. Spread it into a prepared pan and let it cure, uncovered, for at least 4 hours or overnight. Cut and coat as desired. Store the cut marshmallows for up to 2 weeks. Recommended coatings: Cocoa, Cocoa–Ancho Chile, Cinnamon, Gingerbread.

Mint Julep Marshmallows

MAKES A 7 X 11 X 1 ½-INCH PAN

A unique dessert to have for a Kentucky Derby party, fragrant with mint and generously laced with bourbon, these marshmallows will be a big hit whether it's Derby Day or not. If you like a pronounced mint flavor, use 2 cups of mint leaves; otherwise, use 1 1/2 cups.

For the mint puree:

1 1/2 to 2 cups torn fresh mint leaves, lightly packed

3/4 cup water

For the bloom:

3 tablespoons unflavored gelatin

3/4 cup bourbon

For the base:

3/4 cup water

1 1/4 cups Marshmallow Syrup (page 26)

1 1/2 cups granulated cane sugar

Pinch salt

Prepare a pan by coating it with nonstick spray, then wiping it lightly with a paper towel so that only a thin film of oil remains.

First, make the mint puree. Place the mint leaves and water into a blender container and blend until perfectly smooth. Pour the puree into a fine mesh sieve set over a measuring cup and drain off any excess liquid, reserving it to use in the base. Add enough water to the mint liquid to make 3/4 cup. Place the puree in a small bowl.

Next, make the bloom. Place the gelatin in the small bowl with the mint puree and whisk in the bourbon until the mixture is smooth. For the base, place all ingredients along with the 3/4 cup mint liquid into a heavy 4-quart pan set over high heat and bring to a boil. Cover the pan and boil for 2 minutes, then uncover it, insert a candy thermometer, and cook the syrup to 250 degrees F. *Do not stir the mixture once the lid has been removed.* When the base reaches 250 degrees, remove the candy thermometer and stir in the bloom. Pour the mixture into the bowl of a stand mixer, gradually increasing the speed to high, beating for 12 minutes. You can cover the mixer with a clean kitchen towel for the first 3 or 4 minutes to avoid splattering hot liquid on yourself.

Remove the bowl from the stand and carefully fold in the bloom. Spread the marshmallow into the prepared pan, smoothing the top and allowing it to cure for at least 4 hours or overnight. Cut and coat as desired. Store the marshmallows for up to 2 weeks. Recommended coating: Basic.

Making Homemade Marshmallow Fluff

The more people I talk to, the more I'm convinced that a love of marshmallow fluff is one of those deep, dark secrets concealed by many adults. Homemade fluff is smoother and fluffier than the commercial version, and it isn't at all gummy. It's also truly versatile and can be successfully flavored in many ways. Use it as a pretty frosting for cakes or cupcakes, as a filling for sandwiching cookies, or to make an exceptional ice cream sundae. Be sure to check out the section in this book that provides suggested uses for fluff.

Chocolate Cherry Tower with Cherry Fluff.

Making Marshmallow Fluff

Marshmallow fluff varies from regular marshmallows in several ways. It doesn't contain gelatin, it's soft instead of firm, it requires refrigeration no matter what the flavor, and it doesn't need to be cured. Air is beaten into egg whites, and syrup that has been cooked to the firm ball stage or higher is beaten in, "setting" the air-filled whites. The volume of the beaten whites will increase significantly when you beat the base into them. If they can withstand the hot temperature, the flavoring ingredients are cooked with the base; otherwise, they are added to the fluff as it is beating.

Egg Whites—Fresh or Powdered

You have the choice of using raw egg whites or powdered whites in these fluff recipes. Many people shy away from using raw eggs because of the possibility of salmonella, so I've tested all of the fluff recipes using both raw whites and the Just Whites brand of dried egg whites. Don't use meringue powder for these recipes because it contains a lot of other ingredients besides egg whites. The Just Whites brand is 100 percent pasteurized egg whites, is easy to use, and doesn't require refrigeration. One advantage to using the powdered whites is that it is a lot more difficult to overbeat them. Another is that you don't have to separate the whites. Use whichever you prefer.

Fresh Egg Whites

All egg whites called for in these recipes are from eggs graded large. If the eggs you buy aren't graded large, you can measure the whites in a liquid measure. One large size egg white equals 1 fluid ounce. For example, if a recipe calls for 4 large whites, you would measure out 4 liquid ounces of whites from any other size eggs.

It's best to separate eggs when they are cold. Then let the whites sit at room temperature to warm up while you organize the rest of the ingredients and begin making the syrup; whites whip to a larger volume when they are at room temperature. Begin beating them on medium speed (number 5 on a Kitchenaid mixer) when directed in the recipe and keep an eye on them so they don't overbeat (become dry and lumpy-looking) before the base is cooked and cooled.

Powdered Egg Whites

I'm a terrible ingredient snob, so when I decided to test with powdered whites, I was predisposed to thinking the results would be dismal. Boy, was I surprised. None of my taste testers found the fluff less desirable than the ones made with fresh whites, and I found myself reaching for the powdered whites first because they were just easier to use.

Here's how to use powdered egg whites in the fluff recipes: for every egg white called for in the recipe, place 2 *level* teaspoons egg powder and 2 tablespoons *warm* water into a small bowl and whisk for 1 or 2 minutes, until all of the powder is dissolved and there are no lumps. Pour it into the bowl of a stand mixer, beating on medium speed (5 on a Kitchenaid mixer). Start cooking the base as soon as you start beating the whites. You can continue beating the powdered whites at this point until the base is ready.

Storing Marshmallow Fluff

Place marshmallow fluff in a container with a tight-fitting lid and store it in the fridge for 1 to 2 weeks, depending on the recipe.

Freezing Fluff

You can successfully freeze fluff for use as a semi-freddo dessert. It doesn't freeze solid, so it's easily scooped for serving. Let it sit at room temperature for 15 minutes or more before serving it.

NOTE:

Any of the fluff recipes in this book can be doubled.

Vanilla Fluff

The flavor of vanilla comes through clearly in this fluff, so be sure to use a high-quality pure vanilla extract, not imitation. The fluff is versatile and yummy; spoon it on ice cream, spread it on peanut butter sandwiches, or use it to frost cupcakes. It can keep for up to 2 weeks in your fridge, but it will disappear long before that.

For the base:

1/2 cup water

1 1/4 cups Marshmallow Syrup (page 26)

1 1/2 cups granulated cane sugar

For the egg foam:

4 large egg whites, at room temperature, or equivalent reconstituted dried egg whites

1/8 teaspoon salt

Additional flavoring:

2 teaspoons pure vanilla extract

Place the base ingredients into a heavy 2-quart saucepan and bring to a boil over medium heat. Cover and boil for 2 minutes. Remove the cover, insert a candy thermometer, and boil to 240 degrees F. *Do not stir the mixture once the lid has been removed.* Remove the pan from the heat and set it aside to cool for 3 or 4 minutes.

When the temperature of the base reaches 220 degrees F, place the whites and salt in the bowl of a stand mixer and beat on medium speed until thick, fluffy, and opaque. When the base reaches 240 degrees, slowly stream it down the side of the mixer bowl, taking care not to let the base get into the beater so it doesn't splash. Drizzle in the vanilla. Turn the speed up to high and beat for 7 minutes. Transfer the fluff to a plastic container, cover, and store in the fridge for up to 2 weeks.

Cinnamon Fluff

Make Vanilla Fluff (page 84), adding 1 teaspoon ground Saigon (or Vietnamese) cinnamon, or more to taste, during the last minute of beating.

Chocolate-Speckled Fluff

The combination of Vanilla Fluff (page 84) and chocolate shavings tastes like Oreo cookies with a lot of crème filling. Follow the directions for Vanilla Fluff, except cook the base to 260 degrees F. Start beating the whites when the temperature reaches 240 degrees F. When the fluff is finished, fold in 2 ounces shaved semisweet chocolate that has been set in the freezer for 30 minutes or more.

Lemon Fluff

MAKES ABOUT 1 QUART

The fresh, bright flavor of lemon brings an enticing spark to this fluff. Be sure you use fresh-squeezed lemon juice because the bottled kind just doesn't have the same refreshing flavor. Straining the juice before measuring it ensures you'll get just the flavorful juice without the flavorless pulp.

For the base:

1/3 cup water

2/3 cup Marshmallow Syrup (page 26)

2/3 cup granulated cane sugar

For the egg foam:

3 large egg whites, at room temperature, or equivalent reconstituted dried egg whites

1/8 teaspoon salt

Additional flavoring:

1/4 cup strained fresh lemon juice

3/4 teaspoon finely minced freshly grated lemon zest

Place the base ingredients in a heavy 2-quart saucepan and bring to a boil over medium heat. Cover and boil for 2 minutes, then remove the lid, insert a candy thermometer, and turn up the heat to medium high. *Do not stir the mixture once the lid has been removed.* Boil until it reaches 250 degrees F. Meanwhile, place the egg whites and salt in a mixer bowl and beat on medium high until they are thick, fluffy, and opaque.

When the temperature reaches 250 degrees F, turn off the heat, remove the thermometer, and let the base cool for 3 or 4 minutes. Slowly stream the base down the side of the mixer bowl into the beating egg whites, with the mixer on medium-high speed.

Then turn up the mixer to high and beat for 7 minutes. Reduce the speed to medium and add the lemon juice a tablespoon at a time, beating after each addition until the juice is blended in. Increase the speed to high and beat for 1 minute. Remove the bowl from the stand and fold in the zest with a rubber spatula. Transfer the fluff to a covered container and store in the fridge for up to 2 weeks.

Blackberry Fluff

MAKES ABOUT 7 CUPS

I can't wait for the pick-your-own blackberry farms to open—the fruit is so succulent and such a lovely color, and it makes spectacular marshmallow fluff. Use locally grown fresh blackberries in season, or use blackberries frozen without sugar any time of year for the best flavor. It's worth the 5 minutes it will take to remove the seeds with a food mill or a fine strainer, but if you don't have the inclination, the fluff will still have a great flavor. You can also use Perfect Puree's wonderful seedless blackberry puree (see resources, page 173).

For the base:

1/2 cup water

1/3 cup Marshmallow Syrup (page 26)

1/2 cup granulated cane sugar

For the egg foam:

2 large egg whites, at room temperature, or equivalent reconstituted dried egg whites

Pinch salt

Additional flavoring:

3/4 cup + 2 tablespoons seedless pureed blackberries

Place the base ingredients into a 2-quart saucepan set over medium-high heat, stirring to moisten the sugar. Bring the base to a boil, cover, and boil for 2 minutes. Remove the cover, insert a candy thermometer, and cook to 240 degrees F. *Do not stir the mixture once the lid has been removed.*

When the temperature reaches 240 degrees F, put the egg whites and salt into the bowl of a stand mixer and start beating them on medium speed. As they beat, they will become thick, fluffy, and opaque.

When the base is done, remove the pan from the stove and let it cool for 3 or 4 minutes. Stream it into the beaten whites with the motor running on medium speed. Once the base has been added, increase the mixer speed to high and beat the fluff for 7 minutes. Start adding the puree 1/4 cup at a time, beating for 30 seconds after each addition. When it all has been added, beat on high for 3 additional minutes.

Blueberry Fluff

Follow the Blackberry Fluff recipe, substituting blueberry puree for the blackberry puree.

Meyer Lemon and Thyme Fluff

MAKES ABOUT 4 CUPS

Frank Meyer brought Meyer lemons into the United States in 1906 from China. They're a cross between lemons and tangerines, and are a beautiful yellow-orange color when ripe, with sweeter juice than regular lemons. Meyers are available during the winter months. They marry well with thyme, but also try the mint variation. You can make this recipe and omit the herbs altogether, if you prefer.

For the base:

3/4 cup water

1/2 cup Marshmallow Syrup (page 26)

2/3 cup granulated cane sugar

4 generous sprigs fresh thyme

For the egg foam:

3 large egg whites, at room temperature, or equivalent reconstituted dried egg whites

1/16 teaspoon salt

Additional flavoring:

1/4 cup strained freshly squeezed Meyer lemon juice

1/2 teaspoon freshly grated Meyer lemon zest

First, make the base. Place the water, Marshmallow Syrup, and sugar into a 2-quart saucepan set over medium heat and bring the mixture to a boil. Add the thyme, cover, and remove from the heat. Allow the thyme to steep in the base for 30 minutes. Discard the thyme. Bring the base to a boil over medium-high heat, and boil for 2 minutes. Remove the cover and the thyme, insert a candy thermometer, and continue to cook until the base reaches 240 degrees F. *Do not stir the mixture once the lid has been removed.*

As soon as you remove the cover from the pan, place the whites and salt into the bowl of a stand mixer and start beating them on medium speed. They will become thick, fluffy, and opaque.

When the base is done, remove it from the heat and let it cool for 3 or 4 minutes, then stream it into the egg whites, with the motor running. When the base has been added to the whites, increase the mixer speed to high and beat for 4 minutes. Reduce the speed to medium, stream in the juice, increase the speed to high, and finish beating the fluff.

Remove the bowl from the stand and fold in the zest. The fluff will keep, in a covered container, for up to 10 days in the fridge.

Meyer Lemon and Mint Fluff MAKES ABOUT 4 CUPS

Follow the directions for Meyer Lemon and Thyme Fluff, but replace the thyme sprigs with 1 1/2 cups lightly packed, coarsely torn mint leaves, and increase the water for the base to 1 cup.

Espresso Fluff MAKES ABOUT 7 CUPS

Espresso powder provides a deep, superb flavor here. This fluff goes well with any chocolate or vanilla dessert, and a dollop in hot chocolate is simply divine. It makes a wonderful frosting and is delightful on ice cream too. The espresso flavor is strong in this recipe, but if you like it stronger, you can increase the amount of espresso powder.

Additional flavoring:

2 tablespoons espresso powder

2 tablespoons hot water

For the base:

1/2 cup water

1/2 cup Marshmallow Syrup (page 26)

2/3 cup granulated cane sugar

For the egg foam:

3 large egg whites, at room temperature, or equivalent reconstituted dried egg whites

1/16 teaspoon salt

Mix the espresso and hot water in a small bowl until smooth and set the bowl near the mixer.

Place the base ingredients in a heavy 2-quart saucepan set over medium-high heat and bring it to a boil. Cover and boil for 2 minutes, then uncover, insert a candy thermometer, and cook the base to 240 degrees F. Remove it from the heat and let it cool for 3 or 4 minutes. *Do not stir the mixture once the lid has been removed.*

As soon as you put the lid on the base, start beating the whites and salt on medium speed with a stand mixer. They will become thick, fluffy, and opaque. When the base has slightly cooled, stir the espresso mixture into it and then stream it into the egg whites with the motor running. When the base has been added, increase the speed to high and beat the fluff for 8 minutes. It will keep refrigerated for up to 2 weeks.

Butterscotch Fluff

Butterscotch, the combination of brown sugar and butter, is a timeless flavor that follows us through childhood right into adulthood. It complements most chocolate desserts, and tastes sumptuous when topping a bowl of ice cream.

For the base:

3/4 cup water

*1/3 cup Marshmallow Syrup
(page 26)*

1 cup light brown cane sugar

For the egg foam:

*3 large egg whites, at room
temperature, or equivalent
reconstituted dried egg whites*

1/16 teaspoon salt

Additional flavoring:

*1 teaspoon pure vanilla extract
mixed with 1 tablespoon water*

*1 tablespoon unsalted butter
(European style will taste
better here), cut into bits*

Put the base ingredients into a heavy 2-quart saucepan set over medium-high heat and bring it to a boil. Cover and boil for 2 minutes, then remove the cover, insert a candy thermometer, and cook the base to 240 degrees F. *Do not stir the mixture once the lid has been removed.* Then remove the pan from the heat and let the base cool for 3 or 4 minutes.

When you remove the cover from the base, place the egg whites and salt in the bowl of a stand mixer and start beating them on medium speed. They will become thick, opaque, and fluffy.

When the base has cooled a bit, stream it into the whites with the mixer running on medium speed. Drizzle in the vanilla and water and then increase the speed to high and beat for 8 minutes.

While the fluff is beating, slowly melt the butter, leaving a few small bits not melted. Stir the butter until it is smooth and creamy. It's important that it hasn't separated; if it has, redo it.

When the fluff has finished beating, remove the bowl from the stand and gently fold in the butter in 2 parts. The fluff will keep, refrigerated, for up to 2 weeks.

Cherry Fluff

(See photo, page 80.)

When my daughter, Emily, tasted this fluff, she said it reminded her of cherry lollipops. The flavor is mild, not at all overwhelming, and reminiscent of childhood. Pure cherry flavoring has a beautiful, full flavor, unlike extract. Boyajian pure cherry flavor is available in some specialty kitchen shops and online (see reources, page 173).

For the base:

1/4 cup 100 percent tart cherry juice

1 cup Marshmallow Syrup (page 26)

1 cup granulated cane sugar

For the egg foam:

5 large egg whites, at room temperature, or equivalent reconstituted dried egg whites

1/8 teaspoon salt

Additional flavoring:

1/3 cup 100 percent tart cherry juice

1/4 teaspoon pure almond extract

1/2 teaspoon pure cherry flavoring

Place the base ingredients in a heavy 2-quart saucepan and bring to a boil over medium heat. Cover the pan and boil for 2 minutes. Then remove the lid, insert a candy thermometer, increase the heat to medium high, and cook the base until it reaches 260 degrees F. Do not stir the mixture once the lid has been removed. While the base cooks, place the egg whites and salt in a mixer bowl.

When the base reaches 225 degrees F, start beating the egg whites on medium speed until they are opaque and thick, and the beater leaves firm trails in the whites. Mix the flavoring ingredients together in a measuring cup and set aside.

When the base reaches 260 degrees F, remove the pan from the heat and let it cool for 3 or 4 minutes. Stream the base down the inside of the mixer bowl, into the egg whites, with the motor running on medium-high speed. Increase the mixer speed to high and beat the fluff for 4 minutes. Turn the speed down to medium and add the flavoring ingredients a tablespoon at a time, beating until evenly blended after each addition. When the flavoring has been added, turn the mixer to high speed and beat for 1 more minute.

Transfer the fluff to a covered container and store in the fridge for up to 2 weeks.

Orange Flower Water Fluff

My Armenian father instilled in me a curiosity for the cuisine of that country. Orange flower water, which can be found in specialty stores or on the Internet (see resources, page 173), is a common Middle Eastern flavoring agent that possesses a delicate orange flavor with dramatic floral overtones. It pairs well with nuts and dried fruits. If you like, you can spike the orange flavor by folding in a bit of orange zest at the end.

For the base:

1/4 cup orange flower water

1/4 cup water

1 1/4 cups Marshmallow Syrup (page 26)

1 3/4 cups granulated cane sugar

For the egg foam:

4 large egg whites, at room temperature, or equivalent reconstituted dried egg whites

1/16 teaspoon salt

Additional flavoring:

2 tablespoons orange flower water

1 teaspoon finely minced freshly grated orange zest (optional)

Place the base ingredients into a heavy 2-quart saucepan and bring it to a boil over medium-high heat. Cover the pan and boil for 2 minutes. Remove the cover, insert a candy thermometer, and cook the base to 260 degrees F. *Do not stir the mixture once the lid has been removed.* Remove the pan from the heat and set it aside to cool for 3 or 4 minutes. Stir the additional 2 tablespoons orange flower water into the cooling base.

Start beating the egg whites and salt when the base reaches 250 degrees F. They will become thick, fluffy, and opaque. Stream the base into the beaten whites with the mixer running on medium speed. When the base has been added, turn the mixer to high speed and beat the fluff for 7 minutes. Add the zest, if you are using it, and beat for an additional 30 seconds. Store the fluff in the fridge for up to 2 weeks.

Minted Fluff

MAKES ABOUT 5 CUPS

Beautifully colored and full of good mint flavor, this fluff is wonderful spooned over ice cream and drizzled with chocolate. The variety of mint usually found in grocery and produce markets is spearmint, but if you grow mint in your garden, use whatever variety you grow. Use only the leaves and not the stems to get the smoothest and most flavorful mint puree. It is delicious with baked apples or roasted lamb.

For the mint puree:

1 1/2 cups torn fresh mint leaves, lightly packed

1/3 cup water

For the base:

1/2 cup water

1 1/4 cups Marshmallow Syrup (page 26)

1 1/2 cups granulated cane sugar

For the egg foam:

4 large egg whites, at room temperature, or equivalent powdered egg whites and water

1/8 teaspoon salt

To make the puree, place the mint leaves and water into a blender container and blend until perfectly smooth. Pour the puree into a fine sieve and drain off any excess water. Set the puree aside until it's needed.

Place all of the base ingredients into a heavy 4-quart saucepan over medium-high heat until the mixture boils. Cover the pan and boil for 2 minutes. Remove the cover, insert a candy thermometer, and cook the base to 250 degrees F. *Do not stir the mixture once the lid has been removed.*

When the base reaches 220 degrees, start beating the egg whites with the salt on medium-high speed, until they are thick and opaque, and the beater leaves a firm trail in the whites. When the base reaches 250 degrees F, turn off the heat, remove the thermometer, and slowly stream the hot base into the mixer bowl, with the motor running on medium speed, keeping the stream as close to the side of the bowl as possible to avoid splattering the hot base. When the base has been added, increase the speed to high and beat for 7 minutes. Remove the bowl from the stand and fold in the mint puree.

Transfer the fluff to a plastic container, cover, and store in the fridge for up to 2 weeks.

Concord Grape Fluff

Most kids love the taste of grape juice, and this fluff delivers a clear grape flavor. Use it to make peanut butter and "jelly" sandwiches, or make PB & J Parfait (page 128) for a delicious birthday party treat or special dessert.

For the base:

¹/₄ cup water

²/₃ cup frozen grape juice concentrate, thawed, from a 12-ounce can

1 cup Marshmallow Syrup (page 26)

1 cup granulated cane sugar

For the egg foam:

4 large egg whites, at room temperature, or equivalent reconstituted dried egg whites

¹/₈ teaspoon salt

Additional flavoring:

³/₄ cup + 1 tablespoon + 1 teaspoon, or the balance of the 12-ounce can of frozen grape juice concentrate, thawed

First, make the base. Place the ingredients in a heavy 2-quart saucepan, stir to moisten all of the granulated cane sugar, and bring the mixture to a boil over medium heat. Cover and boil for 2 minutes. Remove the cover, insert a candy thermometer, turn the heat up to medium high, and boil the mixture until it reaches 248 degrees F. *Do not stir the mixture once the lid has been removed.*

While the base is cooking, place the egg whites and salt in the bowl of a stand mixer. When the base reaches 235 degrees F, start beating the egg whites on medium-high speed until they are thick, fluffy, and opaque. Leave the mixer running on medium speed. Once the base reaches 248 degrees F, turn off the heat, remove the thermometer, and stream the base into the beaten egg whites. Beat 5 minutes on high speed, reduce the mixer speed to medium, and drizzle in the remaining grape juice concentrate.

When the concentrate has been added, increase the speed to high and beat an additional 3 minutes. Store the fluff for up to 2 weeks in the fridge.

PB&J Parfait with Concord Grape Fluff.

Apple Cinnamon Fluff

Using undiluted frozen apple juice concentrate in this fluff recipe helps to provide a big apple flavor. By infusing the base with crushed cinnamon sticks and adding ground cinnamon to the finished product, a mellow, full cinnamon flavor is developed that won't overwhelm the apple. For the best cinnamon flavor, use Saigon (or Vietnamese) ground cinnamon, which can be found in most grocery stores.

For the base:

1/2 cup frozen apple juice concentrate, thawed but not diluted

1/4 cup water

1 cup Marshmallow Syrup (page 26)

1 cup granulated cane sugar

Three 3-inch cinnamon sticks, crushed and placed in a tea ball

For the egg foam:

5 large egg whites, at room temperature, or equivalent reconstituted dried egg whites

1/8 teaspoon salt

Additional flavoring:

1/4 teaspoon ground Saigon (or Vietnamese) cinnamon

Place the base ingredients, *except the cinnamon sticks*, into a heavy 3-quart saucepan over medium heat, stirring to moisten all of the sugar. Bring the base to a boil and insert the tea ball. Cover the pan, turn off the heat, and let the cinnamon steep for 30 minutes. Remove the tea ball.

Bring the base back to a boil over medium-high heat and boil for 2 minutes. Remove the cover and insert a candy thermometer. *Do not stir the mixture once the lid has been removed.* Cook the syrup to 245 degrees F. While the base is cooking, place the egg whites and salt in the bowl of a stand mixer. When the temperature of the base reaches 230 degrees F, start beating the egg whites on medium speed until they are thick, fluffy, and opaque. Once the base reaches 245 degrees F, turn off the heat, remove the thermometer, and stream the base into the beaten egg whites with the mixer on medium-high speed. Beat the fluff for 8 minutes on high speed, reduce to medium speed, and sprinkle in the ground cinnamon.

Store the fluff in a covered container in the fridge for up to a week.

Banana Fluff

If you love bananas, you'll find it hard not to eat this fluff right out of the container with a spoon. Be sure to use truly ripe bananas—the skins should have lots of dark brown spots, but the banana shouldn't be mushy—so the big banana flavor comes through. This fluff is a delicious fat-free topping for ice cream, chocolate pudding, fruit salads, and cakes.

For the base:

½ cup banana nectar (available in health-food and well-stocked grocery stores)

1¼ cups Marshmallow Syrup (page 26)

1½ cups granulated cane sugar

For the egg foam:

4 large egg whites, at room temperature, or equivalent reconstituted dried egg whites

⅛ teaspoon salt

Additional flavoring:

1½ cups pureed bananas (around 3 or 4 medium bananas)

½ teaspoon Fruit-Fresh, optional (available in most grocery stores)

Place the base ingredients in a heavy 2-quart saucepan over medium-high heat, stirring to moisten the sugar. Bring it to a boil, cover the pan, and boil for 2 minutes. Remove the cover, insert a candy thermometer, and cook to 260 degrees F. *Do not stir the mixture once the lid has been removed.*

Meanwhile, place the egg whites and salt in the bowl of a stand mixer, and start beating them at medium speed when the temperature of the base reaches 245 degrees. They will become thick, fluffy, and opaque. When the base reaches 260 degrees F, turn off the heat, remove the thermometer, and set the base aside to cool for 3 or 4 minutes. Slowly stream the base into the beaten egg whites with the mixer running. When the base has been added, increase the mixer speed to high and beat for 5 minutes.

Meanwhile, place the banana puree in the work bowl of a food processor. Add the Fruit-Fresh, if you are using it, and process until smooth.

When the fluff has beaten for 5 minutes, reduce the mixer speed to medium and add the pureed bananas, a tablespoon at a time. Then increase the speed to high and beat for 3 more minutes. Store in an airtight container in the fridge for up to 2 weeks.

Honey-Star Anise Fluff

MAKES 4 CUPS

Star anise is one of those mystery spices that many people shy away from. That's such a shame because it has a sensuous, captivating taste that melds with many other flavors. Warm, sweet, and aromatic, it's utilized widely throughout Asia, the Middle East, and Northern Africa. Its beautifully formed star shape with tiny seeds peeking out of each of its points has often been the subject of food art. Star anise pairs well with citrus, carrots, pears, figs, and many teas. You need to use a larger pan for this fluff because the honey will make it boil up high. You can replace some of the honey with an equal amount of Marshmallow Syrup if you would like a less pronounced honey flavor.

For the base:

1/2 cup water

3/4 cup honey

1/4 cup Marshmallow Syrup
   (page 26)

1 cup granulated cane sugar

3 whole star anise

For the egg foam:

5 large egg whites, at room
   temperature, or equivalent
   reconstituted dried egg whites

1/8 teaspoon salt

Place the base ingredients into a heavy 4-quart saucepan set over medium-high heat, and bring the mixture to a boil. Remove the pan from the heat, place a cover on it, and let the star anise steep in the base for 30 minutes.

Remove the lid, remove the star anise, and bring the base to a boil again over medium-high heat. Cover the pan and boil for 2 minutes. Then remove the lid, insert a candy thermometer, and cook the base to 250 degrees F. *Do not stir the mixture once the lid has been removed.*

When the base reaches 240 degrees F, beat the egg whites and salt with a stand mixer set at medium speed until the whites are thick, fluffy, and opaque.

When the base is done, remove it from the heat and allow it to cool for 3 or 4 minutes. Slowly stream it into the beaten whites and increase the speed to high. Continue beating for 8 minutes. Store the fluff for up to 2 weeks in the fridge.

Honey Fluff

Make Star Anise Fluff (page 98), using 1 cup honey and no Marshmallow Syrup, and omit the star anise. Try making it with different honey varieties to taste their distinctive flavors. Be sure to use a larger pan for this fluff because the honey causes the base to boil up considerably.

Honey-Lavender Fluff

Honey and lavender go well with many things. Try a small dollop of this on chocolate pudding, or be adventurous and serve a spoonful with aged goat cheese. Be sure to use a 4-quart pan because the honey will cause the base to boil very high.

Make the recipe for Honey–Star Anise Fluff (page 98), omitting the star anise and Marshmallow Syrup, and using 1 cup honey. Place 2 to 3 tablespoons lavender in a tea ball. Bring the base to a boil, insert the tea ball so that the lavender is submerged, cover the pan, and remove it from the heat. Let the lavender steep for 30 minutes. Continue with the Honey–Star Anise recipe from this point, leaving the tea ball in the base until it has finished cooking.

Honey–Star Anise Fluff.

Blood Orange, Rosemary, and Zinfandel Fluff

MAKES ABOUT 6 CUPS

This is my favorite fluff. It's an absolutely lovely rose color with a lively complex flavor. Serve a dollop with grilled chicken or roast pork, or use it to top off stewed figs. It is also excellent with cheesecake. Blood, or Moro, oranges are available through the winter and have a reddish blush on their skins and deep burgundy juice. Use fresh-squeezed for the best flavor.

For the base:

1 cup strained blood orange juice

1 cup Marshmallow Syrup (page 26)

1 1/4 cups granulated cane sugar

1/2 cup zinfandel wine

Four 7-inch sprigs fresh rosemary

For the egg foam:

4 large egg whites, at room
  temperature, or equivalent egg
  white powder and water

1/8 teaspoon salt

Additional flavoring:

1/3 cup strained blood orange juice

2 tablespoons zinfandel wine

1 teaspoon freshly grated, finely minced
  blood orange zest

Place the base ingredients except the rosemary sprigs in a heavy 4-quart saucepan and stir to moisten the sugar. Bring the mixture to a boil over medium heat and add the rosemary sprigs. Cover the pan, remove it from the heat, and let the rosemary steep in the base for 30 minutes. Bring the base to a boil again and boil for 2 minutes. Remove the cover, remove the rosemary sprigs, insert a thermometer, and boil the base on medium-high until it reaches 250 degrees F. *Do not stir the mixture once the lid has been removed.*

While the base is boiling, place the egg whites and salt in the bowl of a stand mixer. When the base reaches 235 degrees F, start beating the whites on medium-high speed, until they are thick, fluffy, and opaque. Once the base reaches 250 degrees F, turn off the heat, remove the thermometer, and allow the base to cool for 3 or 4 minutes. Carefully stream the base into the whites with the mixer running on medium speed. Increase the speed to high and beat for 7 minutes. While the fluff is beating, mix the flavoring ingredients in a small bowl. When the fluff has beaten for 7 minutes, reduce the speed to medium and drizzle the flavoring mixture into the fluff. Increase the speed to high and beat for 1 additional minute.

Lime-Cilantro Fluff

Excellent with angel food cake, or with tropical fruit sorbets, this brightly flavored fluff is refreshing and appetizing anytime.

For the base:

- *1/3 cup water*
- *2/3 cup Marshmallow Syrup (page 26)*
- *2/3 cup granulated cane sugar*

For the egg foam:

- *3 large egg whites, at room temperature, or equivalent reconstituted dried egg whites*
- *1/8 teaspoon salt*

Additional flavoring:

- *1/3 cup strained fresh lime juice*
- *1 teaspoon freshly grated, finely minced lemon zest*
- *1/2 cup finely chopped fresh cilantro leaves*

Place the base ingredients in a heavy 4-quart saucepan and bring to a boil over medium heat. Cover and boil for 2 minutes, then remove the lid, insert a candy thermometer, and turn up the heat to medium high. *Do not stir the mixture once the lid has been removed.* Boil the base until it reaches 240 degrees F.

While the base is cooking, place the egg whites and salt in a mixer bowl. As soon as the lid is placed on the pan, start beating the egg whites on medium-high speed until they are thick, fluffy, and opaque.

When the base temperature reaches 250 degrees F, turn off the heat, remove the thermometer, and allow the base to cool for 3 or 4 minutes.

Slowly stream the base down the side of the mixer bowl into the beaten egg whites with the mixer on medium-high speed. Then turn up the mixer to high and beat the fluff for 7 minutes. Reduce the speed to medium and add the lime juice a tablespoon at a time, beating after each addition, until the juice is blended in. Increase the speed to high and beat for 1 minute. Fold in the zest and cilantro with a rubber spatula. Transfer the fluff to a covered container and store in the fridge for up to 2 weeks.

Chocolate Fluff MAKES ABOUT 5 CUPS

My husband, Michael, loves this fluff; it's creamy and light and has a good chocolate flavor. Serve it with ice cream, puddings, or, as my son, Ben, and my husband do, just eat it by itself. You can use it to make fluffer nutter sandwiches, to top a chocolate cream pie, or to fill tiny tartlet shells to serve with coffee after dinner.

For the cocoa slurry:

1/3 cup excellent-quality cocoa, such as Ghirardelli

2 teaspoons instant espresso powder

1/3 cup boiling water

1 1/2 ounces semisweet or bittersweet chocolate, 52 percent cocoa solids or higher, melted

1 teaspoon pure vanilla extract

For the base:

1/3 cup water

3/4 cup Marshmallow Syrup (page 26)

1 cup granulated cane sugar

For the foam:

5 large egg whites, at room temperature, or equivalent reconstituted dried egg whites

1/4 teaspoon salt

First make the slurry. Place the cocoa and espresso powder into a small bowl and whisk in the boiling water until smooth. Add the melted chocolate and the vanilla, and whisk again until perfectly smooth. Set the slurry near the mixer.

Place the base ingredients into a heavy 2-quart saucepan over medium-high heat. Bring the base to a boil, cover the pan, and boil for 2 minutes. Remove the lid, insert a candy thermometer, and cook the base to 260 degrees F. *Do not stir the mixture once the lid has been removed.*

When the base reaches 235 degrees F, make the foam. Place the egg whites and salt into the bowl of a stand mixer and beat on medium speed. They will be ready when thick, opaque, and the wire beater leaves a trail in them.

Remove the base from the heat when it reaches 260 degrees F and set it aside to cool for 3 or 4 minutes while the egg whites finish beating. Slowly stream the base into the foam while the mixer is set at medium. Then increase the mixer speed to high and beat the foam for 8 minutes.

Remove the bowl from the mixer and gently fold in the slurry with a rubber spatula, being careful not to deflate the fluff. Store the fluff in an airtight container for up to 1 week in the fridge.

Frozen Chocolate Fluff

MAKES ABOUT 3 CUPS

Rich and creamy, smooth and chocolaty, this versatile frozen fluff will be a favorite in your home. After trying out the pumpkin fluff in the freezer, I thought I would give this a try. It's quite seductive; perfect for a warm summer night. Buy high-quality natural cocoa and chocolate for the best flavor. Let the frozen fluff sit out at room temperature for at least 15 minutes before serving.

For the cocoa slurry:

1/3 cup unsweetened cocoa

2 teaspoons espresso powder

1/3 cup boiling water

1 1/2 ounces semisweet or bitter-sweet chocolate (at least 54 percent cocoa solids), melted

1 teaspoon pure vanilla extract

For the base:

1/3 cup water

1 cup Marshmallow Syrup (page 26)

1 cup granulated cane sugar

For the egg foam:

5 large egg whites, at room temperature, or equivalent reconstituted dried egg whites

1/8 teaspoon salt

First, make the cocoa slurry. Combine the cocoa and espresso powder in a medium-size bowl. Add the boiling water, stirring with a small whisk until the mixture is perfectly smooth. Add the melted chocolate and stir again, making sure there are no lumps, then stir in the vanilla. Set the bowl near the mixer.

Place the base ingredients into a heavy 4-quart saucepan, stirring gently to moisten the sugar. Bring to a boil over medium-high heat, insert a candy thermometer, and cook to 250 degrees F. *Do not stir the mixture once the lid has been removed.*

When the temperature of the base reaches 250 degrees F, start beating the egg whites and salt with the mixer on medium speed until they are thick, fluffy, and opaque. When the temperature of the base reaches 260 degrees F, turn off the heat, remove the thermometer, and move the pan away from the stove. Allow the base to cool for 3 or 4 minutes. Stream half the base mixture into the beaten whites with the mixer set at medium and increase the mixer speed to high, beating for 4 minutes. Stir the cocoa slurry into the remaining base.

Reduce the speed to medium and stream in the base/slurry mixture. Immediately increase the speed to high and beat for 8 minutes. Store the fluff in a covered container in the freezer for up to 2 weeks.

Dessert Wine Fluff

MAKES 4 CUPS

Sometimes you are just looking for a simple accompaniment to serve with a favorite dessert. This fluff can be paired with cakes, mousses, or any compatibly flavored dessert. Use a wine that will team well with the dessert you will be serving.

For the base:

1/2 cup dessert wine

1 cup Marshmallow Syrup (page 26)

1 1/4 cups granulated cane sugar

For the egg foam:

4 large egg whites, at room temperature, or equivalent reconstituted dried egg whites

1/8 teaspoon salt

Additional flavoring:

3/4 cup dessert wine

Place the base ingredients in a heavy 2-quart saucepan over medium-high heat, stirring until the sugar has been moistened. Bring the mixture to a boil, cover the pan, and boil for 2 minutes. Remove the lid, insert a candy thermometer, and increase the heat to medium high, boiling the mixture until it reaches 250 degrees F. *Do not stir the mixture once the lid has been removed.*

When the temperature of the base reaches 235 degrees F, beat the egg whites and salt on medium speed, using a stand mixer. They will become thick, fluffy, and opaque. Once the base reaches 250 degrees F, remove the thermometer and set the base aside to cool for 3 or 4 minutes. With the mixer running on medium speed, slowly stream the base into the beaten egg whites. Increase the speed to high and beat the fluff for 8 minutes.

Reduce the mixer speed to medium and start slowly streaming in the 3/4 cup dessert wine. It should take a full minute to add it. Then turn the mixer up to high and beat another minute. Store the fluff in an airtight container in the fridge for up to 1 week.

Poached Pear with Dessert Wine Fluff.

Frozen Pumpkin-Spice Fluff

Pumpkin is a bit heavy for the egg foam to support on its own, but the flavor was so good that I decided to see what would happen if it was frozen. It makes a wonderful dessert served with coffee on a warm fall evening. It's not hard, like ice cream, when frozen; it's soft enough to spoon into bowls. Let it sit at room temperature for at least 15 minutes before serving.

For the base:

3/4 cup apple juice or cider

2/3 cup Marshmallow Syrup (page 26)

1/2 cup granulated cane sugar

1/2 cup light brown cane sugar

For the egg foam:

3 large egg whites, at room temperature, or
equivalent reconstituted dried egg whites

1/8 teaspoon salt

Additional flavoring:

1/2 cup pumpkin puree (canned, not
pumpkin pie filling) mixed with:

1/2 teaspoon ground Saigon
(or Vietnamese) cinnamon

1/4 teaspoon ground ginger

Pinch ground cloves

Place the base ingredients into a heavy 2-quart saucepan over medium-high heat. Bring the base to a boil, cover the pan, and boil for 2 minutes. Remove the lid, insert a candy thermometer, and cook the base to 240 degrees F. *Do not stir the mixture once the lid has been removed.*

When the base reaches 230 degrees F, place the egg whites and salt into the bowl of a stand mixer and beat on medium speed. They will be ready when thick, opaque, and the wire beater leaves a trail in them.

When the base is done, remove the pan from the heat and let it cool for 3 or 4 minutes. Then stream the base into the beaten whites while mixer is set on medium. Increase the mixer speed to high and beat the fluff for 8 minutes.

Remove the bowl from the stand and carefully fold in the pumpkin-spice mixture. The fluff will firm up in the freezer. It will keep for up to 2 weeks.

Green Tea and 5-Spice Fluff

MAKES ABOUT 5 CUPS

Maccha (also spelled matcha) green tea is a finely powdered green tea with a vibrant color and full flavor. It's expensive, but you only need a small amount (see resources, page 173). The Japanese use it for tea ceremonies, and to color the popular dessert called mochi. It blends well with spices and produces a lovely sage-colored fluff. Chinese 5-spice powder is a combination of spices designed to balance the yin and yang of foods. It represents the 5 flavors of Chinese cooking: sweet, sour, savory, salty, and bitter. The exact formula depends on the manufacturer, and some can be spicy—adjust the level you use to meet your own taste. Serve this pretty fluff with fruits, angel food cake, or as frosting for cupcakes.

For the base:

1/2 cup water

1 cup Marshmallow Syrup (page 26)

1 cup granulated cane sugar

For the egg foam:

4 large egg whites, at room temperature, or
   equivalent reconstituted dried egg whites

1/16 teaspoon salt

Additional flavoring:

1 tablespoon maccha tea powder mixed with
   1 1/2 teaspoons Chinese 5-spice powder
   (found with the spices in many grocery
   stores)

Place the base ingredients into a heavy 2-quart saucepan set over medium-high heat and bring it to a boil. Cover the pan and boil for 2 minutes. Remove the cover, insert a candy thermometer, and cook the base until it reaches 245 degrees F. *Do not stir the mixture once the lid has been removed.*

Start beating the whites and salt as soon as the base starts to boil. They will become thick, fluffy, and opaque.

Remove the cooked base from the heat and let it cool for 3 or 4 minutes. Stir the tea powder and spices into the cooling base with a whisk. Stream the partially cooled base into the beaten whites while mixer is set on medium, then increase the speed to high and beat the fluff for 8 minutes. It will keep refrigerated for up to 2 weeks.

Using Homemade Marshmallows and Fluffs

While homemade marshmallows are great eaten out of hand, and home-made fluff makes ice cream seem like a bona fide luxury, there are a lot of ways to enjoy both of them that you might not have yet considered.

Many of your "old favorite" marshmallow desserts are included here, updated using homemade marshmallows and fluff. In addition, you'll find several new ways to use both marshmallows and fluff in impressive yet simple desserts.

Use the recipes for marshmallows or fluff included earlier in the book, or develop your own special flavors to use with the recipes here. Either way, you will find that homemade marshmallows have more uses than you ever imagined!

Chocolate Cupcake Snowballs.

S'mores

Could such a nostalgic food get any better? Yes, it surely can. Homemade marshmallows add a new dimension to s'mores with their warm creaminess, great texture, and delicious flavor. You can make any flavor s'more you like just by varying the flavor of the marshmallows. Use packaged grahams, or the recipe I've included, just in case you'd like to make your own. These s'mores are great when the marshmallows are toasted over a campfire or simply over your grill at home.

Any flavor homemade marsh-
mallows

Milk or dark chocolate bars,
broken into pieces the size
of the grahams

Graham crackers, in squares

Toast marshmallows over a campfire or the heat of an outdoor grill, using long metal or wood skewers. Place a piece of chocolate bar on a graham cracker square and lay the marshmallow on the chocolate. Use a second piece of graham cracker to hold onto the marshmallow while you remove the skewer from it. Repeat as necessary.

Homemade Graham Crackers

For the graham crackers:

³/₄ cup butter, preferably European
style, such as Plugra, at cool room
temperature

¹/₂ teaspoon salt

1 ³/₄ teaspoons baking powder

¹/₄ teaspoon baking soda

¹/₃ cup granulated cane sugar

¹/₄ cup brown sugar

¹/₄ cup mild flavored honey

1 large egg, at room temperature

1 ¹/₄ cups all-purpose unbleached flour

1 ³/₄ cups whole wheat four, preferably
stone ground

For the cinnamon sugar topping:

¹/₂ cup granulated cane sugar

¹/₂ teaspoon ground Saigon (or
Vietnamese) cinnamon

Preheat a conventional oven to 350 degrees F or a convection oven to 330 degrees F. Line 2 baking sheets with parchment paper.

Using an electric mixer, set on medium-high speed, beat the butter, salt, baking powder, baking soda, sugars, and honey for about 3 minutes, or until fluffy and smooth. Add the egg and beat for an additional minute on medium-high speed. Add the flours, beating on low speed just until they are completely blended in, about 30 to 45 seconds. Using a rubber spatula, scrape the bottom and sides of the bowl and give the dough a few stirs to be sure it is evenly mixed. If the dough is sticky, wrap it with plastic wrap, press it into a flat disc, and chill it for 30 minutes.

Roll the dough into a rectangle ¹/₄ inch thick on a lightly floured surface and pierce it all over with a fork. Cut the dough into 3-inch squares; be sure that the dough doesn't stick to the work surface by lightly sprinkling flour under the dough as needed. Move the cut dough squares to the parchment-lined baking sheet and bake them in the preheated oven for 9 to 12 minutes. Completely cool the graham crackers on a wire rack and store them in an airtight container for up to 3 weeks.

Chocolate Cupcake Snowballs

MAKES 24 SNOWBALLS   (See photo, page 108.)

When we think back to the snowballs of our childhood, they always taste much better than the ones we can buy today. Well, these snowballs truly are better. All-natural ingredients and freshly made marshmallow make these treats an absolute delight. Be sure the coconut you use is soft and moist. Spoon or pipe the marshmallow onto the cupcakes, as you prefer. You can color coconut by placing it in a plastic bag with a tiny bit of food coloring and shaking it until the flakes are colored.

Dark Chocolate Cupcakes
  (recipe follows on page 113)
Any flavor fluff your heart desires
4 cups, more or less, shredded or
  flaked sweetened coconut
Pastry bag with a long, narrow, plain
  decorating tip
Any flavor marshmallow batter you
  want to use

Line 2 baking sheets or trays with parchment paper. Make the marshmallow batter *after* the cupcakes are completely cooled, *after* you have made the fluff, and just before you are ready to assemble the snowballs. While the marshmallow batter is being beaten, fill the pastry bag 1/2 full with fluff and insert the tip into the top of a cupcake. Squeeze as much fluff into the cupcake as you can without it oozing out, and turn the cupcake upside down on the parchment-lined tray. Repeat until all of the cupcakes are filled.

When the marshmallow batter is finished, use an offset icing spatula to spread it over the cupcakes as evenly as possible. Sprinkle the coconut all over the marshmallow batter and let the cupcakes sit out for a couple of hours before eating them. They can be made ahead and stored in an airtight container, with a corner of the lid slightly ajar, for up to 5 days in the fridge.

Dark Chocolate Cupcakes

¹/₂ cup unsalted butter, at room temperature

¹/₂ cup Dutch-processed cocoa powder

¹/₂ cup hot water

2 ounces chopped unsweetened chocolate

1 ³/₄ cups cake flour

1 ¹/₄ cups granulated sugar

¹/₂ cup brown sugar, firmly packed

1 ¹/₂ teaspoons baking soda

¹/₂ teaspoon baking powder

¹/₂ teaspoon salt

2 large eggs, at room temperature

1 ¹/₂ teaspoons pure vanilla extract

1 ¹/₄ cups buttermilk, at room temperature

Preheat a conventional oven to 375 degrees F or a convection oven to 350 degrees F. Line the wells of 2 twelve-cupcake pans with paper liners. Set a rack so it is in the center of the oven.

Place the butter, cocoa, and water in a 1-quart saucepan and bring it to a boil. Stir with a whisk until it is thoroughly mixed and remove it from the heat. Add the unsweetened chocolate and stir until it is completely melted.

Measure the flour, sugars, baking soda, baking powder, and salt into a large mixing bowl, and stir with a whisk to combine. Whisk the eggs, vanilla, and buttermilk in a large measuring cup and add to the chocolate mixture, whisking to blend evenly. Stir the chocolate mixture into the dry ingredients, whisking until evenly blended and smooth.

Place a scant ¹/₄ cup of batter in each cupcake well. Bake 1 pan at a time on the center rack in the preheated oven 15 to 18 minutes. The cupcakes will be done when a skewer inserted into the center comes out clean. Remove the pan from the oven and immediately flip it over on a wire rack to release the cupcakes. Turn them right side up and let them cool completely before frosting or freezing.

Rocky Road Brownies

This is a good way to use up any leftover, slightly hard marshmallows you may have hanging around. Homemade marshmallows melt more easily than the store-bought ones, so you need to leave them out, cut into small pieces and uncovered, for 1 or 2 nights. If you don't, they will melt right into the brownie batter. Banana marshmallows are especially good in these brownies.

1 ½ *cups marshmallows, cut into ½-inch bits and left out to harden for at least 24 hours*

2 *tablespoons unbleached flour*

Unbaked batter for Eileen's Deep Chocolate Brownies (page 116)

Peanuts or other nuts, coarsely chopped

Preheat a conventional oven to 350 degrees F or a convection oven to 330 degrees F. Line a 9 x 13 x 2-inch baking pan with foil, and butter the foil.

Toss the marshmallow bits in the flour and fold them into the batter with the nuts. Spread the batter into the prepared pan and bake in the preheated oven for 35 to 45 minutes, or until the brownie is slightly firm when touched lightly in the center with your finger. A toothpick or skewer inserted into the center of the brownie should *not* come out clean. Set the pan on a wire rack to cool for 30 minutes, remove the brownie from the pan and the foil, and set it on a wire rack to cool completely. Cut as desired. Store the brownies in an airtight container, in the fridge, for up to 10 days.

Eileen's Deep Chocolate Brownies

MAKES A 9 X 13 X 2-INCH PAN

You will need to use 2 pans, 1 inside the other, for these rich, dense brownies so the edges don't bake before the center does.

2 ounces unsalted butter

6 ounces semisweet or bittersweet
   chocolate

2 ounces unsweetened chocolate

4 ounces unsalted butter, at room
   temperature

1 cup granulated sugar

$^3/_4$ cup brown sugar, firmly packed

4 large eggs

1 teaspoon pure vanilla extract

$^1/_4$ teaspoon salt

1 $^1/_2$ cups unbleached all-purpose flour

$^2/_3$ cup unsweetened cocoa

Place one 9 x 13 x 2-inch pan inside the other and line the top one with heavy-duty foil. Spray it with nonstick spray or butter it. Preheat the oven to 350 degrees F if you are using a conventional oven or 330 degrees F if you are using a convection oven, and set a rack so it is in the center of the oven.

Melt the 2 ounces of butter with the chocolates, being very careful not to burn the mixture, until most but not all of it has melted, stirring with a fork or whisk until it is completely smooth. Set the mixture aside.

Cream the 4 ounces butter, sugars, eggs, vanilla, and salt on medium-high speed for 4 to 5 minutes, until it is thick, smooth, and light in color. Turn the mixer down to medium speed and slowly add the melted chocolate mixture, continuing to beat for 30 seconds after the chocolate has been added. Scrape the bowl with a rubber spatula and add the flour and cocoa. With the mixer off, stir the flour and cocoa into the batter a few stirs, then beat the mixture on low speed for about 20 seconds. Scrape the sides and bottom of the bowl with a rubber spatula, giving the mixture a few stirs to be sure it is evenly mixed. Pour the batter into the foil-lined double pan and spread it evenly.

Place the pan in the preheated oven on the center rack and bake the brownie 35 to 45 minutes. When it is done, the brownie will feel barely firm to the touch and a wooden pick stuck into the center will come out without any wet batter, although the pick will look wet. The top will be smooth and shiny. Remove the pan and set it on a wire cooling rack until it is completely cool. Cut as desired and store, covered, in the fridge, for up to 10 days.

Dessert Pizza

MAKES ONE 12-INCH PIZZA

Kids love eating sweets that look like dinner. I think they feel like they're pulling one over on the big guys. Using real pizza or bread dough helps to keep this dessert from being overly sweet. Vary the type of fruit you use, and change or omit the candy. You can make the pizza early in the day and add the strawberries at the last minute.

1 package fresh uncooked pizza dough,
or 1 loaf frozen bread dough, thawed

2 cups Chocolate Ganache (recipe follows),
made with half milk chocolate and
half dark chocolate

1 1/2 cups cut-up marshmallows

1/3 cup candy-coated chocolate pieces

1 1/3 cups sliced fresh strawberries

Roll out the dough and bake it according to the package directions. Let it cool completely before assembling the pizza.

Spread slightly warm ganache over the dough, leaving a 1/2-inch rim around the edge. Sprinkle the ganache with the cut-up marshmallows and the candy pieces. When you are ready to serve the pizza, place the sliced strawberries generously around, and if you like, use a propane torch to soften or brown the marshmallows. Cut with a pizza wheel and serve.

Chocolate Ganache

MAKES ABOUT 2 CUPS

Use a top-quality chocolate because it's the flavor of the chocolate that makes Chocolate Ganache so superb. I prefer Callebaut, which is available in some gourmet shops and on the Internet (see resources, page 173). Some other brands worth trying, available in many grocery stores, are Scharffen Berger, Lindt, Ghirardelli, and Valrhona.

1 cup heavy cream

8 ounces excellent-quality
dark chocolate,
chopped small

Scald the cream in a saucepan over medium heat, or microwave it in a large microwave-safe measuring cup on high for 2 to 3 minutes, until a skin forms on the surface. Remove the pan or cup from the heat. Add the chopped chocolate to the cream, and stir *gently* with a wire whisk until the mixture is completely smooth, dark, and glossy. The smaller the chocolate was chopped, the quicker this will occur.

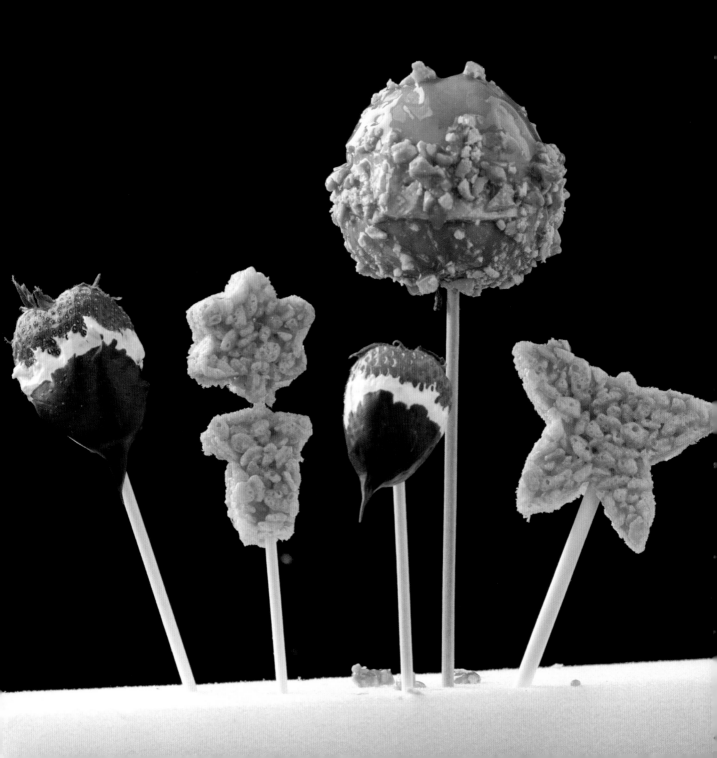

Crispy Rice Treats

MAKES ONE 9 X 13 X 2-INCH PAN

Nearly everyone in the United States has eaten these sweet gems. They've become a staple at bake sales, as after-sports refreshments, or for birthday party delights. You can make them with either fluff or marshmallow, so if you have a little extra of either around the house, this is a great way to use it up. Try using one of the pretty-colored marshmallow or fluff flavors to make your treats more special. You will be the envy of all the other class moms. And there's no wheat or corn in them, either.

3 tablespoons salted butter

7 ounces, by weight, any flavor fluff, or 10 ounces, by weight, marshmallows

7 cups crisp rice cereal

Spray the bottom and sides of the pan or mold with nonstick spray, and wipe lightly with a paper towel so that only a thin film of oil remains on the surface.

Melt the butter and fluff or marshmallows together until smooth. Add the cereal and stir until all of it is evenly coated. Spread into the prepared pan and let sit until cool. Cut as desired and wrap in plastic wrap. They will keep for several days in an airtight container.

Chocolate Chip or Confetti Crispy Rice Treats

Make the recipe for Crispy Rice Treats, above, adding 1 cup of mini semisweet chocolate chips, or 1 cup of candy-coated chocolate pieces.

Fluff and Chocolate-Dipped Strawberries,
Crispy Rice Treats, and Caramel Apple Treats.

Homemade Mallowmars

Mallowmars are from way back in some of our memories. They are graham crackers topped with marshmallow and dipped in chocolate, and are incredibly delicious. Use any flavor marshmallow batter that you like. People are delightfully surprised when they eat homemade mallowmars, but they really go crazy when they are filled with banana, strawberry, or any other unexpected marshmallow flavor. If you don't feel up to dipping the mallowmars, you can just drizzle the tempered chocolate over them decoratively.

Packaged graham crackers or Homemade Graham Crackers (page 111)

Piping bag and plain decorating tip with a 1/2-inch hole

Freshly made marshmallow batter of any flavor

Tempered chocolate (page 147)—made with 1 ounce chocolate for each mallowmar + an extra 12 ounces for ease of dipping

Don't make the marshmallow batter until everything else is ready. If you are using homemade grahams, cut them out into circles before baking them. If you are using packaged grahams and would like to cut them into circles, you'll need to soften them first. To do so, place them on a cutting surface in a single layer and lay a damp kitchen towel over them for several minutes. When they begin to soften, use a round cookie cutter to cut circles out of the squares. Place the circles on a parchment-lined baking sheet and refresh the grahams in a preheated 350-degree-F oven for about 5 minutes.

Pipe a mound of marshmallow batter onto each round and let them cure for 3 or 4 hours before dipping them in chocolate.

Line baking sheets with parchment. Temper the chocolate in a cool, dry room according to the directions given, and place a marshmallow-topped graham on a 2-pronged meat fork, dropping it into the chocolate and gently pushing it under the chocolate to coat it.

Lift it with the fork, tapping the fork on the side of the bowl to remove excess chocolate so you have a thin coating, slide the bottom of the fork across the side of the bowl to remove chocolate drips, and coax the mallowmar onto a parchment-lined baking sheet using a skewer. Repeat for each mallowmar. Let the chocolate set before storing them. They will keep for a few weeks with wax paper between layers in an airtight container.

Chocolate-Espresso Whoopie Pies

Pennsylvania, where I live, is noted for the Pennsylvania Dutch influence in its food. At many of the farmers markets throughout the state, Amish and Mennonite stalls offer home-baked goods that have become synonymous with Pennsylvania Dutch cooking. One of the baked items that you can always find is the Whoopie Pie. It is a cake-like, soft cookie that is sandwiched with a "cream" filling. My family has a joke that these yummy cookies got their name because whenever they were made, the baker's family would yell "whoopie!" This recipe calls for Espresso Fluff, but you can use any flavor you like.

2 cups granulated sugar

1 cup unsalted butter, at room temperature

2 large eggs, at room temperature

2 teaspoons baking soda

1 teaspoon salt

2 teaspoons pure vanilla extract

1 cup cocoa

4 cups bleached all-purpose flour, divided

1 cup sour cream

1 cup warm water

Espresso Fluff (page 89), or any other fluff flavor you desire

Preheat a conventional oven to 375 degrees F or a convection oven to 350 degrees F, and arrange the oven racks so they divide the oven into thirds. Line 2 baking sheets with parchment paper.

First, make the cookie batter. Using an electric mixer, beat the sugar and the butter on high speed until fluffy and creamy, about 2 minutes. Add the eggs, baking soda, salt, vanilla, and cocoa, and beat on medium for about 1 minute, until completely mixed and creamy.

Add 2 cups of the flour and beat on low speed until it is well blended. Add the sour cream and blend well on low speed; scrape the mixer bowl well, add the remaining 2 cups of flour and beat on low speed just until it is mixed in. Scrape the bowl again and add the water, mixing on low speed or stirring with a spatula or spoon, until the batter is smooth and evenly blended. It will be very soft, but that is how it is supposed to be, so don't worry.

Using a 2-tablespoon measure, drop the batter onto the parchment-lined baking sheets, leaving 3 inches between each cookie. Bake the cookies in the preheated oven for about 10 to 12 minutes, reversing the pans halfway through the baking time. The cookies are done when your finger doesn't leave an indentation after lightly touching the cookies.

Remove the pans from the oven and set them on wire racks until the cookies are completely cool. Carefully pull the cooled cookies from the parchment when you are ready to fill them with the fluff.

Turn $1/2$ the cookies upside down on your work surface and place a heaping spoonful of fluff on each cookie, adjusting the amount so that all of the cookies get about the same amount. When this is done, spread the fluff so that it comes to the edge of each cookie, and then cover them with the other half of the cookies.

Whoopie Pies will keep, well covered, for 5 or 6 days refrigerated.

Marshmallow Fluff Fudge

Many names have been given to this recipe, and it has been said that Mamie Eisenhower is the originator. This version is made using homemade Vanilla Fluff (page 84), but you can make it with any fluff flavor you desire. It is creamy, chocolaty, and can be filled with nuts and dried fruits, if desired. This is a good way to use up leftover fluff.

12 ounces good-quality
real chocolate chips

7 ounces fluff (by weight)

1 1/2 teaspoons pure vanilla extract

5 ounces evaporated milk or half-and-half

2 1/2 cups superfine sugar

1/2 cup unsalted butter

1 cup chopped nuts and/or
dried fruit (optional)

Line an 8-inch square pan with foil and spray it with nonstick spray. Place chips, fluff, and vanilla in a large bowl and set it aside.

Heat milk or half-and-half and sugar in a heavy saucepan, stirring constantly, until it boils, then insert a candy thermometer. Boil the mixture to 235 degrees F, stirring constantly to keep it from scorching. Remove from heat and add butter, stirring until it melts; then pour the mixture into the bowl with the chocolate chips, fluff, and vanilla, and stir until smooth. Pour it into the prepared pan, refrigerating for several hours. The fudge will keep in a covered container, in the fridge, for up to 2 weeks.

PB & J Parfait

SERVES 6 TO 8　　　　　　　　　　(See photo, page 95.)

When you want a dessert that speaks to both kids and adults, this is the one to make. It is alternately layered with Concord Grape Fluff and Peanut Butter Mousse, with toasted bread crumbs or graham cracker crumbs sprinkled between the layers for texture. If you don't have clear parfait dishes, you can serve this dessert in a large glass bowl, allowing your guests to serve themselves. The fluff can be made a week ahead, and the mousse a day or 2 before you need it.

Peanut Butter Mousse (recipe follows on page 129)

Concord Grape Fluff (page 94)

¹/₃ batch Concord Grape Fluff, more or less, as needed

3 to 4 slices good-quality white bread, toasted and crushed, or 4 to 5 graham
*　　crackers, crushed*

2 slices white or whole wheat bread, toasted and cut into triangles, or 3 or 4
*　　whole graham crackers, each broken into 4 rectangles*

Peanut Butter Mousse

1 ½ cups heavy cream, well chilled

¼ cup confectioners' sugar

1 ½ cups creamy peanut butter (not the natural kind)

Up to 2 days ahead, beat the chilled cream with the confectioners' sugar until it forms stiff peaks. Place about ¼ of the mixture into another bowl and stir the peanut butter in with a whisk. Then fold the peanut butter–cream mixture into the remaining beaten cream. You can store it in the fridge at this point until the dessert is assembled.

When you are ready to make the dessert, have the mousse, fluff, and crushed toast or grahams all ready to use. Alternate layers of the fluff and mousse, sprinkling a thin layer of crushed toast or grahams between each layer. Garnish with either toast triangles or graham rectangles, depending on what you used between the dessert layers. Store the dessert in the fridge for up to 1 day.

Triple-Treat Brownies

MAKES 15 GENEROUS SERVINGS

Brownies are an all-American favorite and were always a big hit when I had my bakery. The ones used in this dessert have a deep chocolate flavor, a dense fudgy texture, and are not too sweet. Here they are topped with as much or as little marshmallow as you like, given a hit under the broiler so the marshmallow gets soft and browned, and then generously drizzled with caramel sauce. It's like a whole different kind of s'more. Small servings go a long way.

Eileen's Deep Chocolate Brownies
(page 116)

¹/₂ batch or more any flavor marshmallow,
cured in an 11 x 15 x 1-inch pan

Caramel Sauce (recipe follows on
page 132)

Preheat a broiler. Cut the brownie into individual servings and place them on a parchment-lined baking sheet. Cut a marshmallow to fit the brownie and place it on top.

Put them under a broiler for a minute or two until the marshmallow browns, remove the pan from the oven, and set each on a dessert plate. Pour the warm caramel sauce over the top of the marshmallow so that it drips down the sides of the dessert. Serve immediately.

Caramel Sauce

MAKES ABOUT 2 CUPS

My favorite recipe for caramel sauce comes from Barbara Kafka's *Microwave Gourmet* cookbook because it is so easy to make; I've offered an adaptation of that recipe here. If you have refrigerated it, you will need to warm it before it will be thin enough to pour.

1 cup granulated sugar

4 tablespoons cold water

1 cup heavy cream

2 tablespoons unsalted butter

1/2 teaspoon pure vanilla extract

Put the sugar and water into a 4-cup liquid measuring cup that is microwave proof (such as a glass Pyrex measuring cup). Cover the container snugly with plastic wrap and microwave it for about 3 to 5 minutes, or until it starts to turn golden. The amount of time varies according to the wattage of your microwave oven. WATCH CAREFULLY, and check every 30 seconds after you have reached the 3-minute mark, because the sugar will turn from golden to burnt very quickly.

Using an oven mitt, remove the container from the oven and pull the plastic wrap away with a fork so your hand is not too close to the steam. Drizzle the cream in slowly; the sugar syrup will bubble up and may become hard, but don't worry—it will melt again when you return it to the microwave. Add the butter. Place the glass measuring cup in the microwave, uncovered, for 1 minute. Remove and stir to be sure any sugar syrup that hardened is dissolving. Microwave again for 30 seconds, until it is a rich dark brown. If it is not a rich brown, return the syrup to the microwave and repeat in 20-second intervals until the caramel sauce is a deep, rich, caramel brown. Set it aside to cool for several minutes, and then stir in the vanilla. Store the cooled sauce, covered, in the fridge for up to a month. Reheat gently in the microwave when ready to serve.

Caramel Apple Treats

MAKES ABOUT 36   (See photo, page 120.)

A simple and quick treat to make for snack time or as a special item for bake sales, these fun snacks are met with glee by kids (and adults) who love to eat caramel apples in the fall. Everything can be prepared ahead of time and assembled the day they will be served.

Apple Marshmallows (page 48)

Caramel Sauce (page 132)

2 cups chopped roasted peanuts

Wooden skewers

Place an Apple Marshmallow on a wooden skewer and lightly drizzle it with caramel sauce. Roll it in the chopped peanuts and place it on a plate or tray. When finished, wrap the plate with plastic wrap and store the Caramel Apple Treats in the fridge for up to 3 days.

Chocolate Cream Pie

MAKES A 9-INCH PIE

One of the all-time favorites, this pie is luscious as it is, but make it with a marshmallow fluff topping, and people will go wild for it.

Eileen's All-Butter Pastry Crust
(page 138)

Chocolate pudding, chilled

Your favorite fluff flavor

Bake the crust as described in the Banana Cream Pie directions (page 136), and when it is cool, fill it with cooled chocolate pudding. Mound the fluff high onto the filling, and store the pie in the fridge until serving time. It can be made several hours ahead.

Strawberry Shortcake

SERVES 6

Early summer means fresh, intensely flavored strawberries, and there's no better way to enjoy them than in strawberry shortcake. The kind my family eats is made with sweet homemade cream biscuits, not the spongy little cakes sold in the produce section of the grocery store. Try making them—they only take a few minutes—and you won't want to go back to those spongy things. The biscuits are split and filled with sliced strawberries, then topped off with vanilla fluff. Deee-lish!

*1 quart hulled and sliced fresh
    strawberries*

⅓ cup granulated cane sugar

*Sweet Cream Dessert Biscuits
    (recipe follows on page 135)*

*Vanilla Fluff (page 84), or
    your favorite fluff flavor*

Place the strawberries and sugar in a bowl and stir to mix. Allow the berry juices to develop while you make the biscuits. When ready to serve, split the biscuits and spoon strawberries on the bottom ½ of each one. Dollop a spoonful of fluff onto that and set the biscuit tops over the fluff. Spoon some strawberries over the top of the biscuit and place a dollop of fluff alongside the shortcake.

Sweet Cream Dessert Biscuits

These sweet, tender biscuits make great fruit shortcakes, soaking up the juices from the fruit and taking on a creamy, sweet, fruity flavor. They take less than 30 minutes to make, including baking time, so it's simple to put them together for last-minute guests. The recipe can be easily doubled.

1 cup White Lily flour or ½ cup all-purpose flour mixed with ½ cup cake flour

2 tablespoons granulated cane sugar

Pinch salt

2 tablespoons butter, in bits, and chilled

1½ teaspoons baking powder

1¼ cups cold heavy cream

Preheat the oven to 500 degrees F. Process the flour, sugar, and salt in the work bowl of a food processor briefly to mix. Add the butter bits and pulse a few times to evenly mix it in. Slowly add the cream with the motor running, just until the dough starts to hold together. Turn the dough out onto a lightly floured surface and knead it several times to bring it together. Gently roll out the dough into a ½-inch-thick circle and use a sharp 2½-inch cutter to make the biscuits. Place the biscuits on an ungreased baking sheet and set the sheet on the middle rack of the preheated oven for about 8 minutes, or until the biscuits are golden. Serve warm or at room temperature.

Banana Cream Pie or Tartlets

MAKES A 9-INCH PIE OR 10 SMALL TARTLETS

A buttery crust, creamy filling, and fresh banana fluff topping combine to make this dessert a family favorite. Use ripe bananas that have no green on the skin for the best flavor. This dessert is wonderful with coffee after a light dinner.

Pastry Cream (recipe follows on page 139)

Eileen's All-Butter Pastry Crust (recipe follows on page 138)

4 or 5 firm, ripe bananas, sliced

Banana Fluff (page 97)

1 tablespoon lemon juice mixed with 1 tablespoon water, in a small bowl

Make the pastry cream and chill it for at least 3 hours or overnight. Prepare the Banana Fluff. Preheat a conventional oven to 425 degrees F or a convection oven to 400 degrees F.

Make the pastry crust in a 9-inch tart pan or cut the dough and ease it into 10 or 12 small tartlet pans, setting them on a baking sheet. Line the shells with foil and fill them with dry beans or rice. Bake the large crust for 20 minutes or the small ones for 12, then remove the foil and beans or rice and continue baking for another 8 to 10 minutes or so, or until the bottom of the crust is golden. Remove from the oven and cool on a wire rack.

To make a pie: When the crust is cool, spread a third of the pastry cream on the bottom of the crust. Place banana slices over the pastry cream and then spread another third of the cream over the bananas. Repeat, ending with pastry cream, covering it with Banana Fluff mounded up high.

To make tartlets: Fill the pastry shells with pastry cream about half full. Place banana slices over the pastry cream and spread or pipe the fluff on top of the bananas.

Slice a remaining banana into the lemon juice, drain the slices, and set them decoratively into the fluff. The pie or tartlets can be made several hours ahead. Store in the fridge until serving time.

Eileen's All-Butter Pastry Crust

MAKES ONE 9-INCH CRUST

There are many variations of recipes for basic pastry or piecrust, but most of them use shortening for some or all of the fat. Shortening has no flavor and melts above body temperature, so it leaves an unpleasant film in your mouth. If you use good European-style butter, you don't need to use shortening. Crusts made with European butter are easier to work with and will be beautifully browned, flaky, and tender with an absolutely delicious flavor. European-style butter can be found in well-stocked groceries.

The key to tender pastry is to handle it quickly and gently so you don't activate the gluten in the flour. If your hands are warm, dip them in cold water and dry them before handling the dough.

1 cup unbleached all-purpose flour

1/3 cup cake flour (not self-rising)

1 1/2 tablespoons granu-lated cane sugar

1/8 teaspoon salt

5 tablespoons European-style butter, cut into 3/4-inch cubes and chilled

1/4 to 1/3 cup ice water

Place the flours, sugar, and salt into the work bowl of a food processor and pulse several times to mix the ingredients. Add the butter and pulse until mixture resembles large grains of rice. With the motor running, slowly drizzle 1/4 cup of ice water into the work bowl, processing until the dough just begins to hold together. Add more ice water, a teaspoon at a time, if you need to.

When ready to roll out, unwrap the dough and place it on a lightly floured surface. Press the dough down with a rolling pin in several places, then roll the dough from the center to the edge, turning the dough 1/4 turn and repeating until it is the size you want, checking often to see that it isn't sticking to the rolling surface. If it is, sprinkle just a bit of flour under the dough. Fold the dough in half and gently move it to the baking pan, unfolding it and easing it into the corners of the pan. Don't stretch the dough or it will shrink when you bake it.

If your recipe requires a prebaked pie shell, pierce the dough all over with a fork, line the shell with parchment or foil, weigh it down with raw rice or beans, and bake in a preheated 400-degree-F oven on the bottom oven rack for 15 minutes. Then remove the foil or parchment and the rice or beans, and continue baking for another 5 to 10 minutes, or until the bottom is golden.

Pastry Cream

MAKES APPROXIMATELY 1 ½ CUPS

Pastry cream is just a fancy name for rich vanilla pudding. Pastry chefs use it to fill éclairs and tart shells, and as an ingredient in many types of filled cakes and pastries. It's simple to make and will keep for a week or more, so you can make it ahead and assemble desserts at the last minute.

4 large egg yolks

2 tablespoons bleached all-purpose flour

1 cup half-and-half

¼ cup + 2 tablespoons granulated cane sugar

⅛ teaspoon salt

1 ½ teaspoons pure vanilla extract

Lightly beat the yolks in a small bowl and set aside. Place the flour into a heavy saucepan and whisk in the half-and-half until smooth. Add the sugar and salt, and stir to mix evenly. Cook the mixture over medium heat, stirring constantly for several minutes, or until the sauce thickens. Ladle about ½ cup of the hot mixture into the yolks, whisking constantly, then add the yolk mixture to the hot cream mixture, whisking the whole time. Cook over low heat 3 or 4 minutes until the pastry cream thickens. Do not let the mixture boil or it might curdle. Remove from the heat and add the vanilla. Pour into a bowl and press plastic wrap onto the top of the pastry cream so it doesn't form a skin.

Place in the fridge until cold. Stir the pastry cream with a whisk before using.

Neapolitan Chocolate Fondue

SERVES 6 TO 8

Marshmallows and chocolate are a match made in heaven, and here you have 3 delicious flavors of marshmallows to choose from and a luscious chocolate fondue to dip them in. This is about as simple as a homemade dessert can get; the marshmallows can be made days ahead, and the fondue goes together in minutes when heated in the microwave. Set up a tray with the marshmallows arranged on it early in the day, and reheat the fondue just before serving.

Chocolate Fondue (recipe follows)

Chocolate Marshmallows
(page 74)

Strawberry Marshmallows
(page 44)

Vanilla Marshmallows (page 32)

Skewers for dipping

Make the Chocolate Fondue and keep it warm until serving time in a double boiler set over very low heat, making sure the water in the double boiler doesn't evaporate. Alternatively you can make it a day ahead, store it in the fridge, and reheat it very gently in a microwave just before serving time. Arrange the marshmallows around a wide bowl on a tray and set some skewers on the tray. When ready to serve the dessert, pour the fondue into the bowl and serve.

Chocolate Fondue   MAKES ABOUT 3 CUPS

1 pound excellent-quality dark
*   chocolate, cut into small pieces*

2 fluid ounces whole milk

2 fluid ounces orange liqueur or
*   orange juice*

Melt the ingredients together in a double boiler set over barely simmering water, stirring until smooth and then stirring occasionally until serving time.

Orange Crepes with Honey-Star Anise Fluff

SERVES 6 TO 8

You can invite a group over for brunch and be just as relaxed as they are if you serve this dish. All of the components can be made ahead and assembled easily at the last minute.

All you need to add is sausage or bacon, fresh berries, and mimosas for a perfect brunch menu.

Orange Brandy Sauce (recipe follows on page 144)

Sweet Orange Crepes (recipe follow on page 144)

Honey–Star Anise Fluff (page 98)

When it's time to serve brunch, warm the Orange Brandy Sauce in the microwave and remove the platter of crepes from the oven. Serve the sauce alongside the crepes in a bowl with a small ladle or a small pitcher, and serve the fluff in a bowl.

Sweet Orange Crepes

1 cup all-purpose flour

2 tablespoons granulated cane sugar

$1/4$ teaspoon salt

4 large eggs, lightly beaten

$3/4$ cup whole or low-fat milk

$1/4$ cup pulp-free orange juice

$1/2$ cup half-and-half

1 teaspoon vanilla

4 tablespoons unsalted butter, melted

Clarified butter, or nonstick spray, for coating the pan

Beat all of the ingredients together in a mixing bowl until they are evenly blended and there are no lumps. Let the batter sit for 15 minutes before using it. Set a crepe pan or 8-inch omelet pan over medium heat. When the pan is so hot a drop of water sizzles when dropped in it, coat it with clarified butter. (If you are using nonstick spray, you will also need to use a nonstick pan, and be sure to spray it away from the heat source.)

Pour a scant $1/4$ cup of batter into the pan and tilt it in all directions to spread the batter around. Cook a minute or two, turning the crepe when it is golden brown, repeating the same for the flip side.

Stack the crepes on a platter with a paper towel between each crepe, and keep them warm in an oven set to 200 degrees F until needed. Cover the platter with a barely damp kitchen towel so the crepes don't dry out. You can make the crepes a day ahead, store them in a plastic bag in the fridge, and gently warm them in a 250-degree-F oven for about 1 hour the day of your event.

Orange Brandy Sauce   MAKES ABOUT 2 CUPS

Heat $1 3/4$ cups orange juice with 2 tablespoons brown sugar in a microwave until the sugar is completely dissolved. Add $1/3$ cup brandy, or to taste. Reheat for 1 minute at serving time.

Chocolate-Covered Marshmallows

MAKES ABOUT 2 DOZEN 1-INCH CUBES

(See photo, page 146.)

As far as my husband is concerned, there's nothing you can do with a marshmallow that is better than coating it in an excellent-quality tempered chocolate. Tempering chocolate is a matter of realigning the sugar crystals so they are more stable, and results in a smooth, shiny coating that is thin and crisp. The contrast of the thin, sumptuous chocolate coating as it cracks when you bite into it against the soft, creamy marshmallow is a deliriously delicious combination. The directions for simple microwave tempering follow. Do this in low humidity, with the room temperature around 70 degrees or less. If you like, sprinkle a bit of fleur de sel on the top of each marshmallow as soon as it has been dipped. Fleur de sel is coarse-grained sea salt gathered by hand in the Brittany Isles, and can be found in well-stocked grocery stores and gourmet shops.

1/2 batch any flavor marshmallow, cured in 1-inch-high slab

20 ounces excellent-quality dark chocolate

Fleur de sel, if desired

Cut the marshmallows into 1-inch squares and coat them as desired, brushing off as much of the coating as possible. Set a marshmallow on a 2-pronged meat fork, pushing it down into the chocolate so it is coated all over. Lift it out with the fork, and tap the fork on the side of the bowl to remove any excess chocolate, leaving only a thin coating. Drag the fork across the edge of the bowl to remove drips, and set the marshmallow onto a parchment-lined baking sheet, using a skewer to coax the marshmallow off the fork.

Repeat with the remaining marshmallows.

Let the chocolate-covered marshmallows sit on the parchment until the chocolate has set, up to 30 minutes, depending on the temperature in the room. Store then in an airtight container for up to a month in a cool place, away from the sun or heat.

You can also cure the marshmallow in an 11 x 15 x 1-inch jelly roll pan and cut it into fancy shapes before dipping.

Tempering Chocolate in the Microwave

There are many ways to temper chocolate, but this is a truly simple way to do it: place at least 16 ounces of finely chopped high-quality chocolate into a microwave-safe glass bowl; microwave the chocolate until it is about half melted and the chocolate is not more than 110 degrees F. Use an instant-read thermometer to check the temperature. There should still be many soft lumps of chocolate in it.

Remove the bowl from the microwave and stir it with a fork or small whisk until it is smooth. Add about 4 ounces of additional chopped chocolate to the bowl and stir until it melts, continuing to stir until the chocolate drops to 90 degrees F. Wrap a towel around the bowl to help retain the heat, and place the bowl on an electric heating pad set on low that has been covered with a double thickness of kitchen towel.

Drop a marshmallow into the tempered chocolate and, using a dipping fork or a small two-pronged meat fork, lift the marshmallow out of the chocolate by placing the fork under it. Tap the fork on the side of the bowl a few times to force the extra chocolate to drip off, and then scrape the fork over the side of the bowl to remove the extra chocolate from the bottom. Coax the marshmallow from the fork, using a skewer or the point of a sharp knife, onto a parchment-lined baking sheet. Allow the coated marshmallows to set completely before removing them from the parchment and storing them in an airtight container. They will keep for 3 or 4 weeks in a cool place.

Chocolate-Covered Marshmallows.

Baked Alaska

SERVES 8 TO 10

When my son was 8 years old, he asked me to make Baked Alaska for his birthday cake. The idea of a dessert being browned on the outside with cold ice cream inside was a fascination to him. It's simple to make, and you can take it out of the freezer just minutes before you serve it. You'll need a propane torch to brown the tips of the marshmallow covering the Baked Alaska.

Yellow Cake baked in an 8-inch-square pan and cooled (recipe follows on page 150)

2 slices ice cream, each ¹/₂-inch thick, from a ¹/₂-gallon container

Any flavor freshly made marshmallow batter

Make the Yellow Cake according to the recipe and let it cool completely. Slice the ice cream from the long side, to make long, narrow slices, and trim the slices so they fit the slices of cake. Cut the cake into 2 long pieces, and place 1 piece on a serving plate. Top the cake slice with a slice of ice cream, cover the ice cream with the remaining slice of cake, then top that cake slice with the second ice cream slice. Straighten the layers so the sides are even and place the layered dessert in the freezer while you make the marshmallow batter.

When the marshmallow batter has finished beating, remove the layered dessert from the freezer and frost it with the marshmallow batter, using a spatula or knife to make peaks all over the surface. Place the dessert in the freezer until 15 minutes before you are ready to serve it. Just before serving, brown the peaks with a propane torch.

Yellow Cake

3 1/4 cups cake flour

2 cups granulated sugar

1 tablespoon baking powder

1 teaspoon salt

1 1/2 cups milk

2/3 cup unsalted butter, at room temperature

2 large eggs

2 teaspoons pure vanilla extract

Preheat the oven to 350 degrees F and set the oven racks so they divide the oven in thirds. Butter an 8-inch-square pan, line it with parchment paper, and butter the parchment.

Place all of the ingredients into a mixing bowl. Beat the mixture on low speed for 30 seconds, scrape the bowl, and beat the mixture on high speed for 3 minutes. Scrape the bottom and sides of the bowl, being sure to incorporate any unmixed ingredients clinging to the bowl. Spread the batter into the prepared pan. Bake it on a baking sheet in the preheated oven on the bottom rack, rotating the baking pan halfway through the baking time and moving it to the top rack. Bake the cake for 24 to 27 minutes, or until the center springs back when lightly touched, or a skewer stuck into the center of the cake comes out clean.

Poached Pears with Dessert Wine Fluff

(See photo, page 105.)

Belying its ease of production, this great make-ahead dish looks and tastes truly sophisticated. You can make the fluff a week ahead, and the pears can be made 2 or 3 days before you use them. A boldly flavored dessert wine works well in the fluff, but use your imagination and try any wine you fancy. I've made it with Beaume de Venice and Essencia, as well as with zinfandel, all with tasty results.

For the Poached Pears:

6 Bosc pears, ripe but firm, with stems attached

1 bottle Cabernet Sauvignon, or more, as needed

⅓ cup superfine sugar

1 ½ teaspoons freshly grated orange zest

3 sprigs fresh thyme

Pinch salt

For the assembly:

½ recipe Dessert Wine Marshmallow Fluff (page 104)

6 small sprigs thyme for garnish

Peel the pears, leaving the stems attached. Cut a thin slice off the bottom of each pear as needed, to help them stand upright. Place them in a saucepan that is just wide enough to hold them and high enough so they can easily be covered with wine. Pour enough wine into the pan so the pears are completely covered. (It's okay if the stems are sticking out of the wine.) Sprinkle the superfine sugar over the wine, add the zest, thyme, and salt, and bring the mixture to a simmer. Cover the pan and simmer the mixture until the pears are tender when pierced with a fork or small paring knife. Leave the pears in the liquid, and let them cool to room temperature. Store them, covered, in the liquid, for up to 3 days, in the fridge.

Remove the pears from the fridge an hour or two before serving. When ready to assemble the dessert, remove pears from liquid and dry them with paper towels. Drop a generous dollop of fluff onto a dessert plate, and position a pear in the center of the fluff. Garnish with a sprig of thyme and serve.

Dan's Champagne Marshmallow Wedding Cake

SERVES 75 TO 100 GUESTS

When we were working on the photographs for the book, Dan Macey (the food stylist for the photographs for this book) and I were talking about my idea to make small cutouts of wedding cakes as favors for wedding showers. That idea morphed into little stacked wedding cake favors, and then into this actual wedding cake. It's simple to do, and the parts can be made ahead and assembled the day of the wedding. It can be as unfussy or as ornate as you desire, and will definitely be a hit with your guests. Use it as a replacement for a wedding cake, or as a kitschy decoration. Each piece in the cake will serve 2 or 3 guests. The directions below are guidelines; you can cut the marshmallows into any shape you desire, stack and decorate them as you see fit, and use whatever flowers you like. Have fun!

4 batches Champagne Marshmallows (page 59), made in 9 x 13-inch pans (2 batches per pan)

1 or more batches Vanilla Fluff (page 84), depending on how ornate your cake will be

Pastry bag and fluted decorating tube

Pretty plate 14 inches in diameter

Two 8-inch and two 10-inch cake support plates (see resources, page 173)

8 pillars to use with the plates (see resources, page 173)

Shot glasses or other small supports at least 2 inches in height

Cake ornament, if desired

Rose petals or flowers of your choice

To make the cake in the photograph, cut each pan of marshmallow into 4 long 2-inch-wide strips, and then cut each of those strips into 3-inch-long pieces. Cut each of those pieces diagonally into 2 triangles. Coat all of the pieces with Basic Coating (page 27).

Position about $1/2$ of the pieces on the plate for the bottom tier, inserting 3 or 4 small overturned glasses (small shot glasses work well) that are about the height of the marshmallows to support the plates and pillars. Connect the two 10-inch plastic cake-support plates using 4 of the plastic pillars, and center them over the bottom tier, resting on the glasses.

Arrange the marshmallow pieces for the second tier on the top 10-inch plate, using about ²/₃ of the remaining marshmallow pieces, again inserting 3 or 4 small glasses for support. Connect the two 8-inch support plates using the remaining 4 pillars, and center them over the second tier, resting on the glasses. Position as many of the remaining pieces of marshmallow as are needed for the top tier, placing an overturned glass in the center for the cake ornament. Using the pastry bag and decorating tube, pipe decorations as desired onto the marshmallows with the fluff.

Arrange rose petals or flowers on the support plates, and place a dollop of fluff on the support for the cake ornament. Position the ornament on the glass, and enjoy!

When serving the marshmallows, an elegant accompaniment is a small cup of melted chocolate or ganache (page 118) for each guest for dipping.

Hot Chocolate with Cinnamon Mocha Marshmallows

MAKES 1 CUP   (See photo, page 67.)

No mixes allowed here. Steaming, thick, and deeply chocolaty, this warm drink is made the way it is in Europe—with real dark chocolate melted into hot milk. You can increase or decrease the amount of chocolate in each cup, depending on how rich you like your hot chocolate. Elaine Gonzales, queen of chocolate, advises that really good hot chocolate needs to cook for a long time. Cook this for as long or short a time as you like. The marshmallows add a lovely bit of spice and just a touch of coffee to round out the flavors.

1 cup whole milk

3 1/2 ounces chopped bittersweet
   chocolate (more or less, to taste)

Pinch salt

2 or 3 Cinnamon Mocha Marshmallows
   (page 66)

Heat the milk to scalding over medium-high heat, stirring constantly. Reduce the heat to low and add the chopped chocolate and the salt, stirring with a heatproof spatula until the chocolate melts. Continue cooking the mixture, stirring every few minutes, for at least 5 minutes, or as long as you like. Pour the hot chocolate into a mug and top with the marshmallows.

Chocolate Cherry Cake Towers

MAKES 8 SERVINGS

(See photo, page 80.)

Stacked desserts are fashionable and elegant. The parts for this one can all be made ahead and assembled the day of your event. The chocolate cake is dark and moist, and couples brilliantly with the cherry fluff. Dark chocolate ganache flows down from the top of the tower over the sides, drenching the dessert in chocolaty goodness.

Two 11 x 15 x 1-inch baking pans

Baking parchment

2 tablespoons melted butter for brushing pan

2 to 3 tablespoons flour for dusting pan

Unbaked batter for Dark Chocolate Cupcakes (page 113)

Cherry Fluff (page 91), or any other flavor you prefer

Chocolate Ganache (page 118)

Maraschino cherries with stems, well drained and set on paper towels, for garnish

Preheat a conventional oven to 350 degrees F or a convection oven to 330 degrees F. Spray 1 pan with nonstick spray and line the bottom with parchment. Brush the parchment and sides of the pan with butter, and dust it thoroughly with flour. Turn it over and tap out any excess flour. Place it inside the other pan.

Pour the cake batter into the prepared pan and bake for 25 to 30 minutes, until a skewer stuck into the center of the cake comes out clean. Cool on a wire rack for 5 minutes, then turn out the cake onto another wire rack, and flip it over so it's right side up. When completely cool, the cake can be wrapped and frozen for up to 2 months.

Not more than 4 hours before serving time, level the cake if necessary, and cut it into 6 pieces along its length and 4 pieces along its width. Stack the squares with fluff between them, and place the stacks on a tray, using 3 squares per serving. Cover loosely with plastic wrap and set in the refrigerator until serving time.

Make the ganache up to a week ahead and refrigerate it. Gently heat it in a microwave until it's pourable. When it is time to serve the dessert, place each stack on a serving plate, pour ganache over the top so that it oozes down the sides, and top with a cherry.

Doing Fun and Funky Things with Homemade Marshmallows

The easiest and most fun thing to do with marshmallows is to put them on sticks. Hobby and craft stores carry lollipop sticks in different sizes and some even carry them in colors. You can also buy clear cellophane bags in the craft stores. To enclose the marshmallow, twist the bag closed below the marshmallow, and then tie a lovely ribbon around it, leaving the lollipop stick unwrapped to use as a handle. There is no end to what you can do with this concept; I've described a few ideas here to get you started.

Fluff and Chocolate-Dipped Strawberries

(See photo, page 120.)

Look for large, beautifully shaped, and deeply colored strawberries with bright green leaves. Wash them and let them dry completely before you coat them. They will keep for a few hours, but you cannot make them a day ahead because the strawberries will start to weep. You will need to use an extra 12 ounces of chocolate so it can retain its temperature while you dip.

1/2 ounce high-quality chocolate per straw-berry, + 12 ounces for tempering

Lollipop sticks

Fresh strawberries, washed and absolutely dry

Styrofoam or a fresh pineapple cut in half lengthwise

Your choice of fluff

Temper the chocolate according to the instructions on page 147. Poke a stick into the stem end of a strawberry, coat it $^3/_4$ of the way up with the fluff, leaving the stem end uncoated, and then dip it into the chocolate. Push the other end of the lollipop stick into a piece of Styrofoam or a pineapple half that has been placed cut side down. Keep in a cool place, but not refrigerated, until ready to serve.

Crispy Rice Treats to Go

(See photo, page 120.)

Whether it's for a birthday party, a bake sale, Halloween treats, or just to have around, cute cutouts of Crispy Rice Treats on sticks are always appealing. The treats can be made with tinted or fruit-flavored fluff or marshmallows to give some color and unexpected flavor to them.

You can leave them plain, or roll them in multicolored sprinkles, coconut, nuts, or colored sugar. Form them into balls, cut them into cubes, or shape them into upside-down cones, snowmen, or ghosts. This project can keep kids busy for hours. It's a great group project for kids' clubs and can be used as a fund-raiser for them too.

Crispy Rice Treats (page 121) spread into 9 x 13 x 2-inch
and/or 11 x 15 x 1-inch pans, or other pan(s)
of your choice

Some leftover fluff to use as glue

Cookie cutters

Table knives to cut the Crispy Rice Treats for hand shaping

Simple molds such as espresso cups or shot glasses

Colored sprinkles and sugars

Coconut (to dye coconut, see instructions, page 112)

Small candies to use as eyes, buttons, etc.

3-D food-coloring tubes

Chopped nuts

Lollipop sticks

Cellophane bags

Ribbon to tie the bags

Use the cutters to cut desired shapes from the cooled crispy Crispy Rice Treats, and have the kids decorate them as desired. You can scoop out a piece of the treats, to be rolled into a ball similar to a popcorn ball. Roll them in colored sprinkles, chopped nuts, or mini chocolate chips. Or press the treats into lightly oiled molds, carefully pull them out, and embellish.

After they are decorated, insert a lollipop stick into the shape, if desired, put it in a bag, and tie it with a ribbon. Fill a large basket with the beribboned bags and set them out for display.

Have a Marshmallow

Holiday Cutouts and Molded Marshmallows

(See photo, page 158.)

This is where you can really have some fun with kids. There are a multitude of cookie cutters, silicone molds, and small cake pans that can be used to cut or mold marshmallows. Gingerbread people, snowmen, flowers, bunnies and other animals, airplanes, houses, and cars are just some of the fun shapes kids love to make. Advise parents ahead of time to send an oversize shirt for their kids to wear so they don't mess up their clothes.

Marshmallow slabs that have been molded in 11 x 15-inch baking sheets and cured, in various colors and flavors

Marshmallow batter that has been piped into mounds, snakes, and other shapes, and/or into assorted molds, and cured

Freshly made marshmallow fluff or Marshmallow Syrup (page 26), for use as glue

Assorted cookie cutters

A few cupcake pans

Decorating Party!

Assemble your choices of:

Marshmallow coatings
(pages 27–30)

Colored sugars

Food-coloring pens

3-D food-coloring tubes (these
make the marshmallows
look very cool)

Sprinkles and/or jimmies

Coconut, nuts, shaved
chocolate, chocolate chips

Small candies to use as
buttons, eyes, mouths, etc.

Lollipop sticks and cellophane
bags, if you like

Bags or gift boxes for everyone
to transport their creations

Have everything ready when your guests arrive. Place several cupcake pans around the table, with decorations in the wells so they have lots of choices. And no obsessing—let them be creative. It doesn't matter if things don't look perfect.

Having some molded marshmallows along with the marshmallow slabs that they will cut makes it more interesting for the kids. You can pipe batter into oiled shot glasses, piping the marshmallow in wavy tops, to unmold as ghosts that they can paint scary faces on. There are a lot of cake pans in the craft shops and many grocery stores that have small, shaped wells for individual jack-o'-lanterns, happy faces, gingerbread men, snowmen, and other fun and festive shapes. Be sure you allow time for the marshmallows to cure and set well before decorating time.

Help them cut out the shapes they want, and coat them in a coating mixture or colored sugar, or encourage them to select a molded marshmallow. They can easily decorate them with food-coloring pens that are available in grocery and craft stores. Glue candies on for decoration using the fluff as glue. The 3-D food-coloring tubes make neat faces and designs that pop out at you. Use coconut for hair, small candies for special effects. Let their imaginations run wild and have fun.

Wedding Shower Favors

You can make really sweet little favors shaped like wedding cakes out of marshmallows to give at wedding showers. There are 2 ways, and I'll give them both to you. Each makes a lovely and popular gift, and can be made days ahead, boxed and beribboned, ready for your guests' enchantment. They can be made with any flavor or color marshmallow you desire, and look fabulous decorated with 3-D colored icing tubes.

The first favor is a cutout of a wedding cake that lies flat. It's made with a cookie cutter shaped like a tiered cake. It can be decorated as you desire, placed in a gift box or a cellophane bag, and tied with a decorative ribbon. It makes a delightful favor.

The second one is an actual tiny tiered cake made out of 3 sizes of marshmallow circles cut out and then stacked and decorated. Tuck it into a gift box and tie it with a festive ribbon. All of your guests will be charmed. Sources for specialty cookie cutters can be found on page 173.

To make either of them you will need:

Marshmallow batter of any flavor that has been spread into 11 x 15 x 1-inch pans

Cookie cutters: wedding cake shape for the flat favor, or 3 circular cutters for the tiered favor, 1, 2, and 3 inches in diameter

Fluff, if you are making the tiered favors, to glue the tiers together

3-D colored icing tubes in white or colors

Marshmallow Syrup (page 26), for glue

Specially shaped candy cake decorations—flowers, etc.

Boxes and ribbons for packaging

For the flat favors:

Unmold a marshmallow slab from the pan onto a lightly oiled surface, leaving the slab upside down so the tops of the cakes will be smooth. Using the wedding cake–shaped cookie cutter, cut out as many cakes as you can from each marshmallow slab, turning the cutter around to fit into all of the spaces as you go along. Place the cake cutouts onto lightly oiled baking sheets, and when they have all been cut out, use the 3-D colored icing tubes to decorate them with swags and swirls.

Use the food-coloring as glue to attach flowers and other decorations. Let the cakes dry overnight before boxing them.

For the tiered favors:

Cure the marshmallow batter in either a 9 x 13 x 2-inch pan or an 11 x 15 x 1-inch pan, depending on how high you would like each tier to be. Turn out a marshmallow slab onto a lightly oiled surface, keeping it upside down so the tiers have a smooth surface. Cut out the same number of pieces of each of the three circle sizes using oiled cutters, and lay them on lightly oiled baking sheets. Spread the bottom of a 2-inch circle with a bit of fluff and gently press it onto a 3-inch circle. Then spread some fluff on the bottom of a 1-inch circle and gently press it onto the 2-inch circle, creating a 3-tiered "cake." Repeat until all of the circles have been stacked. Decorate with the 3-D colored icing tubes and attach flowers or other decorations, using Marshmallow Syrup for glue. Let them sit out overnight to dry. When they are completely dry, they can be boxed.

Dice

You can make these any size or color. If you want jumbo dice, you'll need to cure the marshmallow batter in a pan that is as deep as you want the dice to be high. They're fun to place at table settings for a casual dinner, and are a conversation piece with dessert. Choose a flavor that will go with your dessert and serve them on the side, place a small pair of dice on the saucers when serving coffee. You can also serve them as a snack when playing Yahtzee or Call My Bluff. Decorate them with letters if you'll be serving them while playing Boggle. If serving them at a dice game, place a pair of marshmallow dice on a small plate or napkin for each player.

Marshmallow batter cured in an
appropriately sized pan

Coating of your choice

Plastic or metal ruler

3-D food-coloring tubes

Turn the marshmallow batter out of the pan onto a surface sprinkled with the coating you will be using for the dice. Carefully cut the dice into cubes, using a ruler to guide you.

Coat the cubes in the coating and shake off as much as possible. Using a 3-D food-coloring tube, make dots on each side corresponding to the dots on the sides of a die. You will have to leave 1 side blank while the other 5 sides dry, then you can go back and add the dots to the last side of each die.

Chick Peepers

It's really easy to make your own little chick "peepers" out of homemade marshmallow batter. You can make them in assorted colors and flavors, or use vanilla with colored sugars.

Gift boxes of assorted flavors make a lovely Easter basket treat. For instructions on piping, see page 20.

Freshly made marshmallow batter, your choice of color or flavor

Piping bag and ³/₈-inch plain decorating tube

3-D food-coloring tube

Coating of your choice or fine colored sugars

Prepare a surface by spraying it with oil and lightly wiping it, or by sprinkling it with a coating mixture. Holding the piping bag so the tip is at a 45-degree angle to the surface, pipe a mound, then push the bag back and up to form a neck, giving a slight extra squeeze to form the head. Dip the finger and thumb of your free hand in water and pinch off the end to form the beak, gently pushing it down, if necessary. Sprinkle with colored sugar and allow to cure overnight, or allow them to cure for a few hours and coat them with your choice of coating. You can place the coating in a bag with some of the peepers and shake it to coat them. Be sure to brush off any excess coating.

Use a 3-D food-coloring tube to paint eyes onto the peepers. Pack them into gift boxes and tie with pretty ribbons.

Favorite Cone Treats

My siblings and I used to buy marshmallow-filled cones at the penny candy counter of our small town's drugstore. They were tiny cones with a firm marshmallow filling. Small cones filled with fluff or marshmallow in assorted colors and flavors make a delightful and festive presentation for family parties, picnics, and birthdays.

You have the choice of making the filled cones with fluff or marshmallow batter. The fluff will stay soft; the marshmallow batter will firm up. Use different flavors and colors for an attractive display.

You can make small cones yourself by carefully chipping away the top portion of sugar cones with a pair of scissors until you get to the size you want. It doesn't matter if the cone has a slightly ragged edge because it can be covered with the filling. The chipped parts of the cones can be used as topping for ice cream, so don't throw them away. Have the cones and the Styrofoam tray ready before you make the fluff or marshmallow batter so it can be piped in when it's fresh. For information on how to use a piping bag, see page 20.

Ice cream cones

Freshly made marshmallow batter(s) in your choice of color and flavor, or freshly made marshmallow fluff(s) in your choice of color and flavor

Piping bag and fluted decorating tube

Styrofoam to hold the filled cones

Multicolored sprinkles, jimmies, or cake decorations, if desired, to sprinkle on the tops

Use a wooden spoon to poke holes into the Styrofoam in an even pattern to hold the cones, being sure to leave enough room between them so the cones are not crowded.

Hold a cone in one hand and the piping bag in the other, and pipe the fluff or marshmallow batter into the cone, moving the tip of the bag in circles to create a swirled pattern, making the circles smaller as you go higher out of the cone. Make a point at the top by pulling up on the bag and releasing the pressure from your hand at the same time.

Decorate the top with sprinkles or jimmies, if desired, and set the cone into a hole in the Styrofoam. The fluff cones should be kept in a cool place until serving, and should be served the same day they are made. The marshmallow batter cones can be left out at room temperature, and will keep for several days.

Resources

Boyajian, Inc.

www.boyajianinc.com

Pure flavorings and citrus oils.

Coffee Gallery

www.CooksShopHere.com

Maccha tea powder.

Fante's Kitchen Wares Shop

www.fantes.com

Cookware, molds, gel food coloring, baking ingredients, colored sugars, cake supports, pastry bags and decorating tubes, cookie cutters, and baking equipment.

King Arthur Flour Company

www.KingArthurFlour.com

Baking ingredients, unsweetened cocoa, chocolate, cookie cutters, molds, espresso powder, dried egg whites, colored sugars, and flavorings.

A. C. Moore Craft Shops

www.acmoore.com

Visit the Web site for store locations.

3-D food color tubes, food color pens, molds, lollipop sticks, cake supports, colored sugars, food coloring gels, and candy gift boxes.

Michael's Arts and Crafts Store

www.Michaels.com

Visit the Web site for store locations.

3-D colored icing tubes, food color pens, molds, lollipop sticks, cake supports, colored sugars, food coloring gels, and candy gift boxes.

Just Tomatoes, Etc.

www.JustTomatoes.com

Freeze-dried fruits and vegetables.

Wilderness Family Naturals

www.Wilderness FamilyNaturals.com

Freeze-dried fruits.

Penzeys Spices

www.Penzeys.com

See Web site for a store in your area, or order online.

Spices, dark cocoa, vanilla, dried chile peppers.

The Perfect Puree of Napa Valley

www.perfectpuree.com

Frozen fruit purees in a variety of flavors, by mail order.

Big Tree Farms

www.bigtreebali.com

Long pepper, wonderful sea salts, and exotic honey flavors.

Green, Aliza. *Field Guide to Produce.* Philadelphia: Quirk Books, 2004.

Green, Aliza. *Field Guide to Herbs & Spices.* Philadelphia: Quirk Books, 2006.

Use these books to find useful information on all kinds of fruits and vegetables, and herbs and spices, as well as information on what flavors go well together.

Index

Metric Conversion Chart

Liquid and Dry Measures

U.S.	Canadian	Australian
¼ teaspoon	1 mL	1 ml
½ teaspoon	2 mL	2 ml
1 teaspoon	5 mL	5 ml
1 tablespoon	15 mL	20 ml
¼ cup	50 mL	60 ml
⅓ cup	75 mL	80 ml
½ cup	125 mL	125 ml
⅔ cup	150 mL	170 ml
¾ cup	175 mL	190 ml
1 cup	250 mL	250 ml
1 quart	1 liter	1 litre

Temperature Conversion Chart

Fahrenheit	Celsius
250	120
275	140
300	150
325	160
350	180
375	190
400	200
425	220
450	230
475	240
500	260